CELIA'S EYES

B ANZ   CR

Anzalone, Celia Marie.
Celia's eyes

WITHDRAWN

4/13

A Life of Love,
Drugs, and Redemption

CELIA'S EYES

CELIA MARIE ANZALONE

TATE PUBLISHING
AND ENTERPRISES, LLC

Citrus County Library System

Celia's Eyes: A Life of Love, Drugs, and Redemption
Copyright © 2012 by Celia Marie Anzalone. All rights reserved.

No part of this publication may be reproduced, stored in a retrieval system or transmitted in any way by any means, electronic, mechanical, photocopy, recording or otherwise without the prior permission of the author except as provided by USA copyright law.

Scripture quotations marked (BBE) are from *The Bible in Basic English*, C.K. Ogden, Cambridge University Press, 1965. Public domain in the United States.

Scripture quotations marked (CJB) are taken from the *Complete Jewish Bible*, copyright © 1998 by David H. Stern. Published by Jewish New Testament Publications, Inc. www.messianicjewish.net/jntp. Distributed by Messianic Jewish Resources. www.messianicjewish.net. All rights reserved. Used by permission.

Scripture quotations marked (HCSB) are taken from the *Holman Christian Standard Bible*®, Copyright © 1999, 2000, 2002, 2003 by Holman Bible Publishers. Used by permission. *Holman Christian Standard Bible*®, Holman CSB®, and HCSB® are federally registered trademarks of Holman Bible Publishers.

Scripture quotations marked (MSG) are taken from *The Message*. Copyright © 1993, 1994, 1995, 1996, 2000, 2001, 2002. Used by permission of NavPress Publishing Group.

Scripture quotations marked (NASB) are taken from the *New American Standard Bible*®, Copyright © 1960, 1962, 1963, 1968, 1971, 1972, 1973, 1975, 1977, 1995 by The Lockman Foundation. Used by permission.

Scripture quotations marked (NCV) are taken from the *New Century Version*®. Copyright © 2005 by Thomas Nelson, Inc. Used by permission. All rights reserved.

Scripture quotations marked (NIV) are taken from the *Holy Bible, New International Version*®, NIV®. Copyright © 1973, 1978, 1984 by Biblica, Inc.™ Used by permission of Zondervan. All rights reserved worldwide. www.zondervan.com.

Scripture quotations marked (NLT) are taken from the *Holy Bible, New Living Translation*, copyright © 1996. Used by permission of Tyndale House Publishers, Inc., Wheaton, Illinois 60189. All rights reserved.

This book is designed to provide accurate and authoritative information with regard to the subject matter covered. This information is given with the understanding that neither the author nor Tate Publishing, LLC is engaged in rendering legal, professional advice. Since the details of your situation are fact dependent, you should additionally seek the services of a competent professional.

The opinions expressed by the author are not necessarily those of Tate Publishing, LLC.

Published by Tate Publishing & Enterprises, LLC
127 E. Trade Center Terrace | Mustang, Oklahoma 73064 USA
1.888.361.9473 | www.tatepublishing.com

Tate Publishing is committed to excellence in the publishing industry. The company reflects the philosophy established by the founders, based on Psalm 68:11,

"The Lord gave the word and great was the company of those who published it."

Book design copyright © 2012 by Tate Publishing, LLC. All rights reserved.
Cover design by Kristen Verser
Interior design by Lynly D. Grider
Cover photos by Alex McMahan Photography

Published in the United States of America
ISBN: 978-1-61862-161-0
1. Biography & Autobiography, Religious
2. Body, Mind & Spirit, Spirituality, General
12.01.26

Dedicated to:
Those that stayed, the ones that never thought to leave,
for "I love you" could not be said a better way.

CONTENTS

Introduction	**13**
This Is Where the Healing Begins	**17**
The Return to Innocence	17
Sylvia Plath	19
Suicide	20
Rock Bottom	21
Self-medicating	21
Full Again	23
Trust	24
Present	26
Get Real	**29**
Fake	29
True Acceptance	31
Light of My life	32
Childhood Interrupted	**35**
Life Isn't Always Fair	35
How Did I Get Here?	35
Messy Divorce	36
Bright Side	38
Outcast	39
Neglect	41
Defensiveness	42
The Wall	42
My Mom	44
Another Bright Side	45
Spiritual Warfare	46
Blamed God	47
Lack of Balance and Stability	49
Dealing with the Bitter Parts	50
Hate	51

He Never Left My Side	52
Feeling Lost? So Was I	**55**
Male Attention	55
Modesty	56
Cutting	58
Being sneaky	59
Runaway Train Wreck: Part One	59
Inpatient Stay	60
The Diary	61
Runaway: Take Two	63
Busted	65
Oppression and His Protection	66
God's Mercy	67
Love and Other Drugs	**69**
First Love	69
The Unhealthy Ones	70
I Remember You, Do You Remember Me Too?	71
Any Form of Abuse Is Not "Okay"	72
First Scare	73
Passive-Aggressive	73
Closure	74
Marijuana and Rumors	75
The Devil	77
My Nonna	81
Meth	82
Rickey Revisited	83
What Goes Up Must Come Down	83
Jesus Loves the Bad Girls, Too	**85**
Help	86
Waking Up	86
God at Work	87
That Night	88
Saw a Doctor	89
Panic/Fear Attacks	89
What Did God Have to Say?	91

Final Wake-up Call	92
Church	93
Just Face It	95

Forgiveness, Compassion, and Divine Intervention — 97

Forgiveness	97
The Door Incident	99
The Day After	102
Spiritual Warfare	103
Wrong One and Wrong Time	105
Bright Side	106
Graham and Sharon	107
The Gift of Compassion	108

Fight for Your Freedom — 109

Get Back with Yourself	110
Double-mindedness	112
Friends	113
Clarity	116

Honor Your Parents — 117

My Dad	117
Pain Validated	119
Mommy Judy	119
My Mother	122
Compromise	123
A Little Grace	124
Grow Up	125
Do Better	126
Take Responsibility	127

Always Seek the Bright Side — 129

Feeling Good	130
Failure	131
Fear	131
Dear God, I Hate Sin	135
Noise	135
Purity	135

Heart Restoration	136
Soul Restoration	137
Holy Spirit Healing	138

My Heart — 141

Guarding My Heart	141
The Desires of My Heart	142
Breakups	144
A Need to be Validated	145
No More Selling Myself Short	145
Pursue God-centered Relationships	147
Letting Go	148
The Toughest	149
Marriage	151
My Future	152

Loving Myself — 155

Perfectionism	156
I Love You	157
Shame	158
Forgiving Myself	159

The Trinity — 161

Intercessory Prayer	161
Jesus	162
God	162
The Holy Spirit	163
The Holy Spirit Baptism vs. the Kundalini Awakening	165
Draw Near to God	169

His Calling — 171

How He Pursued My Heart and Won — 175

The Favorite	175
He's There for Me	176
Connection	176
He Makes Me Feel Special	177
He Makes Me Feel Healthy	178
He Fills Me	179

He Protects Me	180
He Accepts Me Just as I Am	181
His Love Spell	181
He Put My Broken Pieces Together	182
He Leads Me	183
He Has Patience with Me	184
One Wish	184
More of Our Love	**185**
Letter between Us	185
Our First Story	186
Our Second Poem	187
No More Weary, Teary Eyes, Just Sunny Skies	**191**
Remembering Him	191
Other Pursuits	192
Happy, Healthy, Whole	193
His Love	194
His Promise	194
Want Him	195
Note from the Author	**199**
"Celia's Eyes"	203

INTRODUCTION

Those who loved you and were helped by you will remember you when the forget-me-nots have withered. Carve your name on hearts, not on marble.

Charles Spurgeon

To my new friend,

I'm not sure what you are normally up to around 1:00 p.m. on a Friday afternoon, but that is when it all began for us. The date was January 21, 2011, when I was listening to my praise and worship music and felt led to start writing my never-ending thoughts on paper. It was from that moment on that everything in my life began to change, while everything on the outside remained the same.

Now I know I will be writing for the rest of my life.

So you know, I never asked for this nor was it planned. After all, my prayers weren't about you back then; they were all about me. I didn't even know who I was writing that day, but now it's clear.

I was writing you.

The tears began to pour down my face. What I was writing was coming from a heart that was crying out to God on your behalf. His presence drew near to me, and all I could do was pour my heart out through my written words to an invisible audience He had placed in my heart. When I reached a stopping point, I took a moment to review what I had written.

Although surprised at what I had read, I couldn't deny that I had written it. It had been written from my heart, with my very own hands. I couldn't say He had written it as much as I wanted. But I can say He inspired every bit of this.

I know He placed the calling in my heart. For what the calling would require of me, I would've never chosen to pursue on my own.

After seeking counsel, I elaborated on the message. I found myself with over 30,000 words written to you in less than three days. I felt inspired to relive moments of my past for the first time since they occurred, memories which had been suppressed for years.

And I still had so much left to share with you.

The process was therapeutic. I awakened painful parts of my past that weren't completely healed by acknowledging them and giving them their proper respect, a voice to be heard. Did you know that writing you healed my heart? Well, now you do.

I released tears from the innocent little girl that once existed, tears from the broken and battered woman of years past and tears of the confused young girl I was—who was unsure if I would ever become the healthy woman that I so desperately desired to be.

Although I knew becoming transparent could help you, I had no idea what getting real would do for me.

When I came to the end, I realized I had revealed my entire heart to you. At that point I began to second-guess myself and His calling because I felt nervous. What if you were to reject my heart? Besides, shouldn't you have to pursue my heart first? Isn't that what guarding our hearts is all about?

"Above all else, guard your heart, for it is the wellspring of life" (Proverbs 4:23, NIV).

I believe you should always allow others to see your heart; you should just be careful on who you allow to touch it. So although I am giving you my heart for His purposes, I know He still has my heart in His care. It is safe and protected, and I am shielded from any further pain, whatever you choose to do. You can reject my heart, disregard it, or accept it. But it is yours. He told me to give it to you because He loves you that much.

I don't know if you're a believer in Christ or not, but I am. And as a Christ follower, He is my role model. When I was seven years old, my Momaw Swafford told me about what He did for me on the cross. I cried my heart out as I sat at her dining room table inquiring more about Him.

It hurt my heart that He had to suffer for my sake. I instantly connected with Him because He did that for me. And my feelings were also hurt that people took it to the extreme in which they had. I was forever touched and inspired by His love for others, and I truly believe God's Holy Spirit has been with me ever since that day.

Jesus sacrificed His life for all of mankind. How could one not trust that what He said He believed with his entire existence? That is why most people respect His teachings. Whether they let Him in their hearts and accept Him as their Savior or not, they know His words came from His very own heart. I hope He is in yours because I love your soul, and I want to see you saved if you aren't already.

I pray that you take to heart what I say in my message addressed to you. You are about to know me better than I ever knew myself before I began writing you. You will find that if you are hurting, you have a friend in Jesus, and you also have a friend in me. We are all in this thing together because I assure you, dear friend, you are never alone. And sometimes, I know that knowledge is all we truly need.

With love,
Celia

THIS IS WHERE THE HEALING BEGINS

Don't be afraid to be weak; don't be too proud to be strong. Just look into your heart, my friend. That will be the return to yourself, the return to innocence.

Partial Lyrics to "Return to Innocence" by Enigma

THE RETURN TO INNOCENCE

While hoping and hanging on by a thread, I never would have dreamed of the life I live today. My life is the way it was before all of the darkness came upon me as a child, but even better. I can recall as a child feeling this beauty, the beauty of innocence.

I had no earthly idea what I could be. There was no way I could realize my true potential when I was dying inside. The light at the end of the tunnel was too far away. In fact, I couldn't even see my tunnel; I had only heard that there was one. I didn't have any visible proof, no success story to relate to. I had nothing. I didn't even have myself. I only had hope that there was something greater than me to get me through, something greater than myself to revive me back to life.

My mind could barely even recall the past feelings of freedom in Christ that I felt as a child. The loud and clear voice of Satan's lies telling me that I had done too much and was too far gone for repair, that I was a lost cause and worthless were all I could hear after turning my back on the Lord. My actions during this time reflected my core beliefs about myself.

The beliefs came first, the actions followed.

I wanted to be free from things that I didn't want to do. I wanted to be free from things that I was desperately drawn to that were going to kill me if I didn't stop. I was a train wreck waiting to happen. And that wreck happened, all right, in the form of eight car accidents in less than a three year span—four of which were totaled. Thank God for His strength to keep my family behind me and unconditionally loving me during that time of my life.

When I wasn't filling the void with drugs and codependent relationships, the emptiness I felt inside was unbearable. It was more than just a feeling inside that left me feeling ugly or unimportant. I was left with a feeling that I was nothing at all. The only feelings that made me feel alive were the things I was drawn to that made me feel disgusting, mistreated, and abused on every level. But at least then you feel alive, right?

That is why I understand cutters.

Although I was never tough enough to really do it well, I did try many times. A cutter has an identity, and so does the "bad girl." We were created to be known and to know others, and I had no idea who I was. And out of the alternatives that I knew, cutting was better than feeling nothing.

For years, my only dream was to be free. It was a dream that my soul just wouldn't allow to die. But although I dreamed of freedom, I never believed my dreams would one day come true.

Now, I am a believer in fairy tales.

SYLVIA PLATH

In Sylvia Plath's *The Bell Jar*, she talked about her severe depression, which ultimately led to her suicide. I felt a darkness come over me while reading it when I was thirteen years old. Although I was already depressed, I found depression attractive after reading her book. The book fed my depression with its dark and heavy nature.

> *To the person in the bell jar, blank and stopped as a dead baby, the world itself is the bad dream.*
>
> Sylvia Plath, *The Bell Jar*, Chapter 20

She was relatable and transparent, much like my style. But the major difference was she lived deceived by Satan and died deceived by the same. What could her readers learn from her misery? What did she learn? She only made me feel less alone, but I didn't learn how to make my pain go away. And sadly, neither did she.

I could relate to pain and suffering such as Sylvia Plath's. I could feel the overwhelming pressure, even at thirteen that she felt as an adult. The pressure came from the confusion, indecisiveness and the realization that one day, I would need to know who I was. I was lost, and so was she.

> *I wanted each and every one of them, but choosing one meant losing all the rest, and, as I sat there, unable to decide, the figs began to wrinkle and go black..*
>
> Sylvia Plath, *The Bell Jar*, Chapter 7

After researching, I found that the book has actually been banned from schools in the Warsaw, Indiana, area as well as challenged by many others because of its dark content. It was thought to have provoked some of its readers to commit suicide after reading. If someone were already on the edge, I can only imagine how the depressing nature enticed them to take it one step further.

There are just certain things we shouldn't read or watch. There is violence and abuse, a harsh reality. But is it something you would want to subject your child to if you have one? I would say not. How about yourself? I would say that you shouldn't unless you have to, because God wants your heart and mind pure as well.

Because of how her book affected me, I debated on how much I would reveal to you. Not for my sake, but for yours. But then again, my story is unlike Sylvia Plath's. For starters, I lived through my past. I did not die, and there is a very happy ending. There is so much light in my life now that all the darkness from my past is drowned out.

What *The Bell Jar* did not offer was a way out. She did not refer her readers to a better "way" of living. *The Bell Jar* didn't direct you to Jesus.

Jesus answered, "I am the way and the truth and the life. No one comes to the Father except through me" (John 14:6, NIV).

SUICIDE

Several years after entering depression, I ultimately found myself addicted to love and addicted to drugs. I would have rather risked my life and suffer the physical and emotional scars than to face the feeling inside of me that I felt when I was alone and sober. The sickening feeling was too unbearable. That feeling that I ran from made me want to die. I'll never forget all the times I have closed my eyes dreaming of death.

I never let myself experience the ache inside me for too long when I knew I could avoid it. I believe that is why I never felt led to formulate a plan to end my life like many others. Besides, where I was headed an active suicide wouldn't have been necessary due to my addictions nearly taking my life for me on more than one occasion. With that said, I truly understand what could drive a person to commit suicide. I know what it is about.

No matter what struggles or sorrows may come my way, I am excited about living now. I will never pray to die again because I will never ever feel that low. What caused me to feel that emptiness has no authority in a life surrendered to Him. What causes that in you, if you are there, is something that can be remedied. When you embrace all of God, Jesus, and His Holy Spirit, I promise you will never dream of death again.

ROCK BOTTOM

I met my deep dark pit on more than one occasion. The only advantage to the second pit is that on the outside, I seemed to have it more together, and I wasn't lying in my bed coming off of drugs without any sort of hospitalization.

The first time my soul was rotting, second time I felt my heart was dying, and the last was a long time coming.

No one can tell me one pit was worse than the other or that there is only one true rock bottom. My expertise is based on personal experience; you can't top that kind of knowledge. I am bold about what I know, and I have known pain.

SELF-MEDICATING

Why did I find myself addicted to drugs at nineteen years old? Because I hated the way I felt when I was sober. When I was sober I felt my reality. And I chose to run from reality rather than face the fact that I hated what I was doing—I hated the way I looked outside and how I felt inside. The only time I didn't feel the madness that made me driven to hurt myself was when I was giving in to it.

Why did I suffer severe abuse and manage to escape, only to return four days later at the age of 21?

The answer isn't because I truly loved the man I would months later receive an annulment from. If it were true love, I wouldn't have come back after only four days. I would have loved him from a distance while he got help. The fact that I came back before he got help only enabled his behavior. When I stayed, my actions said to him: "I accept your abuse, and I will continue to put up with it." We were walking addictions feeding off of each other. I can't deny I played a part in our demise.

The true reason I stayed is because I needed him to feel whole. When we were together, it made the feeling that I had when I was alone miraculously go away. The emptiness would be filled, but what was causing that void was still there. The feeling was only being masked, buried rather. The emptiness I felt inside always had a way of showing its ugly head, no matter how long and how far I ran.

After all, where can you truly go to escape from yourself?

When a part of someone's body is wounded, what do they usually do? They seek help, apply medication, and give it time to heal. And when something hurts us internally, by choosing to "self-medicate" rather than release the pain through biblical strategies, we are doing ourselves a disservice. For that is running from reality and not addressing our wounds.

What destructive forms of self-medication or bypassing the pain, as I call it, did is actually make the hole I was "medicating" and had been doing it for years. I needed good, sound advice from a male. And since I didn't have that kind of access to my real dad when I needed him, I started seeing Mr. Harris.

My employer paid for six visits a year. So from November 2009 to December 2009, I went nearly every week totaling six visits. And then, the following year I went once every two months.

Between my visits with Mr. Harris, topics would come up that I felt needed some addressing to a professional counselor. I would write them all down in a notebook. The first time I made a list, this is a summary of what I read off to him as things I felt were "issues." This was over three years after finally quitting the drugs I was addicted to, but my mind was still in the process of resetting from all the damage inflicted.

I told him about me emotionally latching onto others who felt safe. I knew it was dysfunctional, but I couldn't stop clinging. I didn't know how to form healthy relationships with men because I didn't even know what it looked like. The reason I was ever involved with them was to have someone father me.

I was in constant fear of rejection from everyone. I was codependent and I was lonely. I didn't have many Christian friends who could lift me up spiritually. I was in the process of rebuilding a life, but I hadn't gotten very far. I told Mr. Harris everything that I felt was dysfunctional about myself and that I felt needed to be fixed. And I told him that I wanted to change.

He would always listen intently to what I had to say. He never looked at me like I was crazy, but with compassion, as he would often pass me a box of tissues. He recommended books, listened and gave me good advice.

Then, one day he told me that he wasn't rushing me out of therapy, but that he wanted to remind me that it wasn't something I would need forever. He told me he thought I had proven to myself that I wouldn't let my life spin out of control again, since he knew that was one of my fears.

At that point, I realized it was time to move on from counseling on a regular basis, and it was time to trust myself again. But before that happened, I had to prove to myself I could be trusted to make sound decisions before I finally stopped second guessing myself.

Learning to trust myself again has been one of my last deficiencies to overcome. And trusting yourself is crucial to living your life whole.

If you don't trust yourself, you are constantly second guessing yourself and looking for other's advice and approval over your own. Seeking counsel when it comes to making decisions is wise. But, not being able to make a decision for fear you don't have the ability to do so on your own isn't a healthy place to be.

PRESENT

Currently, I am a well-rounded twenty-five-year-old who people would never believe has done the things I have. I am fun-loving, bold, and I can be loud. When I meet others, they usually love me or hate me. There's no middle ground unless they flat-out ignore me. And if they chose to hate me, it wouldn't be because I didn't try to win them over. For that is one of my greatest assets and biggest flaws, people pleasing.

I am attracted to depth and character in others. I am drawn to inner beauty more than physical appearance, but I am still human. I can appreciate the beauty in all of God's creation: men, women, children, the elderly, the sky, nature, you name it. I believe in miracles, spiritual warfare, and that it is better to have loved and lost than to have never loved at all.

My life is all sunny skies for the most part these days. Mother Theresa said smiling was a gift you can give to strangers, and I believe she is right. I know they mean a lot to me when I receive them. I have learned there is always something to smile about and that laughing really is the best medicine. I have also learned that healthy God-centered relationships are good for the soul as well.

I am fortunate to have a support system in my life that consists of my family and some close female friends. Although there are some men out there that I love as brothers, I don't keep them as close as the girls anymore. As I have gotten older, I've realized that opposite sex friendships require more boundaries. And I have also learned that when one person is falling and the other isn't reciprocating, it isn't healthy nor is it any fun to remain close friends.

I don't enjoy drama or complications, so I avoid them. But I am not passive-aggressive. If there is an issue, I don't hesitate to confront it right then and there. There are many that I have met and gotten close to in my life that are dear to my heart and always will be, regardless of our level of communication. You know who you are, and you know that I love you forever and always. But very few even know me well enough to where I feel known by them.

And that would be the price I have been willing pay in order to hide my past.

> *Too scared to face all your fear; so you hide but you find that the shame won't disappear. So let it fall down; there's freedom waiting in the sound.*
>
> Partial lyrics to "The Healing Begins" by Tenth Avenue North

GET REAL

What keeps us from being who we truly are with those around us? Why do we so often hide behind a mask? The simple answer is fear.

Mark D. Roberts, *Dare to Be True*

FAKE

The past few years, I have been having a lot of fun working in overdrive to play catch-up with the rest of my peers. I finally "made it" in the world's eyes for my age. And I finally met my dad's standards when I graduated college in December of 2009. That was my rite of passage into earning his approval.

I look awesome "on paper." I'm healthy, attractive, a college graduate, no obvious baggage, nice resumé, and a soon to be published author. But how have I felt on the inside up until now? Fake.

For so long, I have been working and working to get well. Faking it until I could make it.

Becoming real and revealing the truth about where I have been was a challenge because I wanted to please everyone. If I pleased everyone, they would like me. If I am liked, I get to feel that positive feeling that comes along with being liked by others. The feeling of acceptance isn't painful; it feels amazing.

Some of those closest to me and who I care for the most, outside of my family, have absolutely no idea what my story looks like.

I told someone I smoked pot before, and they nearly fell over in shock. My last date even called me "sheltered" to his buddies.

Honestly, I was quite pleased with all of the above. My goal was to keep the ugly parts of my past hidden, and I succeeded. I am considered a "good girl" in the eyes of those who don't know my past, and I have their respect. But no one really knows who I am because not many know where I have been. And out of those I've confided in, even they don't know the whole story.

While I had successfully hid my story away, I had even been hiding from it. I feared others rejection of who I was because I didn't even accept it, the past that has made me into the woman I am today. I protected it by keeping it locked up where no one could see and judge. If no one saw they had nothing to judge. If I presented someone other than myself, the rejection wasn't as damaging.

I feared people looking at me in disgust. I feared people treating me differently. I feared their pity. I feared people knowing my secrets. I feared losing respect in their eyes.

I was so afraid of what others thought because for as long as I can recall, their opinion mattered more to me than my own. Up until now, I only knew what I was worth from what they would tell me with their words and actions. If they told me I was pretty, I would smile. And if their actions toward me said I was unworthy of their time of day, it triggered the most intense pain. I have allowed others to define me my whole life.

My fear of being rejected by others wasn't ever worth the risk to be known. That fear has kept me from reaching out to help others, maybe even you if you were once in any of the shoes I have worn over the years. That fear has been holding me back for as long as I can remember, but not today.

You gain strength, courage, and confidence by every experience in which you really stop to look fear in the face.

Eleanor Roosevelt

TRUE ACCEPTANCE

I am sure there may be some who will be opposed to me speaking my truth so freely. But the only people I truly fear judgment from are all fully behind me, which makes my life that much easier. My family is supportive, and my father even said he was very proud of me for reaching out to others. But most importantly and above all, God led me to do this as a testimony to glorify Him. And His opinion reigns in my life.

My past isn't something I am proud of, and I know it has brought a lot of shame and heartache upon my family. But by not being truthful with others about where I have been, I am being deceptive. And even though my deception keeps me from potential rejection, it also keeps me from true acceptance because I haven't ever been truly known. And I am at a place where I would rather be rejected for who I am than loved for whom I am not. If something isn't real, it's not the truth. And if it's not truth, it's a lie. I only want true acceptance from here on out.

Be who you are and say what you feel because those who mind don't matter and those who matter don't mind.

Dr. Seuss

LIGHT OF MY LIFE

The only way to see the intensity and the power of the light in my life is if I allow others to see the depth of the darkness from my past. One has to see both to fully comprehend how far I have come. And if there are those out there who are hurting now, they need to see that kind of healing power. They need to know it doesn't always have to be that way. There is a way out.

I felt led to share what others might find relatable. I know I was not alone in my suffering. I know I am not the only one out there whose heart has been broken and trampled upon. My heart wants others who have been where I have to know that their soul can be free and their hearts can be healed, no matter what the messages say that are playing in their heads.

Whether you've trusted Jesus in your heart by now or not, you will understand why I believe after reading this. And I hope you also see that change is possible because you will know how I was changed. If you are already a believer, I hope my story inspires you to chase, pursue, and press in to Him. Only by doing that will you ever experience all the gifts He wants to give His children of the Light.

> *"For you were once darkness, but now you are light in the Lord. Live as children of the light."*
>
> (Ephesians 5:8, NIV)

The little insights I will share along the way are my treasures. I only obtained these insights through my suffering. Had I not suffered, I would be without them. I didn't even recognize my treasures until the Light was turned back on in my life. And I never knew what to do with all of them until now. The following verse I relate to very much.

"And I will give you treasures hidden in the darkness—secret riches. I will do this so you may know that I am the Lord, *the God of Israel, the one who calls you by name."*

(Isaiah 45:3, NLT)

CHILDHOOD INTERRUPTED

It's never too late to have a happy childhood. But the second one is up to you and no one else.

Regina Brett

LIFE ISN'T ALWAYS FAIR

My mom and biological dad divorced when I was two-years-old. They were both remarried by the time I was three. I don't remember crying as I chased my dad's car down the neighborhood street when he moved, but I'm certain my heart does.

He moved to Pennsylvania with his new wife, and they started a family. He flew me up three times a year, and we stayed in touch. He has always been emotionally available, and I am blessed that I have that because a lot of women don't. When I was little, we would talk on the phone a lot and I would fall asleep on him. To this day, although I don't see him physically very often, I treasure our phone calls.

I can tell my dad anything. He often feels more like a mentor than a dad. But at least I know him, whether it is in the way I deserved to know him growing up or not, it is the way I was given. And it's in a way that I have grown to accept.

HOW DID I GET HERE?

It all started with a lot of major pain that I didn't understand or know how to process at twelve-years-old. I blamed God and told

Him to go away because I thought my mom's erratic behavior was all God's fault. After all, I was told it was God who baptized her in the Holy Spirit and it was God who was driving her to go from church to church having her demons cast out in front of me.

I wasn't feeling loved. And I was told God was in charge of it all. I wanted nothing to do with what I was seeing, and I didn't have the skills at the time to process the events. I didn't know how to differentiate what was God and what wasn't. And the truth is, what I hated wasn't really Him at all.

At first I became very melancholy, but then I started rebelling to hurt others while hurting myself in the process which was self-destructive. I was spoiled, and I had entitlement issues. I was a wounded little girl, but I kept up a tough exterior. My motto as a young teen was adopted from Bob Dylan, "I don't break the rules because I don't see any rules to break. As far as I'm concerned, there are no rules."

MESSY DIVORCE

My mother had been in a ten-year marriage to a man that was my "dad" from the time my mom and real dad separated at two-years-old until my mom and ex-dad filed for divorce when I was twelve. He would get drunk, manhandle, and threaten to kill her if she left on several occasions. I was scared when they would fight and so were my siblings. I would console my baby brother during the fights when he would cry on the staircase because we would hear and see it all. We should have never had to witness those fights.

I was afraid and constantly felt like I was walking on egg shells around him. I would get yelled at for even licking my lips too much because he said I would make them chapped. There were spankings to the point of bruises on a few occasions. He French-kissed me on the mouth while drunk when I was a toddler in front of my mother. And he encouraged being sexy as a child. I believe the parts of our relationship that were very inappropriate negatively impacted my ability to relate to the opposite sex once I hit puberty.

After my mom got baptized with the Holy Spirit and was behaving erratically, many fights over issues concerning God arose. One day my ex-dad even pushed her out the front door in her church dress to shut her up. My mother was very controlling and fights on Sunday mornings usually occurred over him deciding he didn't want to go to church.

There was always screaming and yelling about getting a divorce. I talked with my teachers about it growing up and they just put it off as normal so I accepted it as the same. Then one day as I was leaving for school, they said they were getting a divorce but little did I know they were going to go through with it. My ex-dad took me and my brother and sister to school and from that day on life was not the same.

I think back to what I was so confused about for so long. Even though I pretended to hate him when they divorced, I loved him. He bought me a gold "Daddy's Little Girl" necklace that I used to wear, and he escorted me when I won second runner-up in Little League homecoming, along with the other dads. He helped coach my softball team, and he was the only dad I have known on an everyday basis. He also walked me down the aisle when I went in front of the church to publicly dedicate my life to Jesus at our Baptist church. Although I knew I had my real dad in Pennsylvania, he was the only dad I truly knew growing up.

I am not sure why we didn't bring much of our things when we had to leave our house. I believe that I didn't because I was in denial. It was all such a blur. I still remember what I was wearing the day the judge finally made his decision in the ex-dad's favor after three months of waiting. It was tough on me, but I didn't shed a tear at the time. However, I am still in the process of grieving thirteen years later since I chose to hold it inside at the time.

The ex-dad was awarded the house with the in-ground swimming pool, my four-wheeler, and all the other toys including the bass boat, full custody of my brother and sister, alimony, child support, and $80,000 for part of the furniture building from the divorce. All my mom received from their divorce was the furniture business that she had jointly bought with him from my popaw when they first got married. I wasn't fought over like my brother and sister, but I'm sure she considered herself blessed to at least still have me during that time, although she never showed it.

When he immediately remarried, upon my mom's research she discovered she no longer had to pay him alimony. That money quite possibly could have aided in the funding of him starting up his own furniture store as competition less than ten minutes away as soon as the divorce was final. Eventually her successful business went down the drain due to his competition and all the hateful rumors that were spread about her by him and his new wife.

BRIGHT SIDE

I was no longer given everything I wanted when her business went under. I was no longer popular. All that mattered to me, regardless of whether it should have mattered or not, was being destroyed. Where was my port in the storm? The whole world felt like it was crashing down on me and it felt that no one really cared about how the turn of events were affecting me. There wasn't any compassion shown, or asking if I was okay. Everyone who once had full access to my heart was breaking it. So I let my pain turn me bitter and cold toward my family.

But a bright side to her losing her business is that although I grew up being spoiled during my younger years, the rest of my days growing up were of valuing money more than I would if I had stayed on that same spoiled path.

Money doesn't buy happiness, nor can it buy character. I am not saying having money means I won't have either of those, I am just saying I would not be the woman I am today if my life had continued down the path of being given everything I wanted. No matter where I am financially, when I have a child I will teach them certain financial principles and not overdo it with the expensive gifts simply because I can.

OUTCAST

When my mom and my ex-dad were going through the second custody battle for my brother and sister, it got really messy. My ex-dad and his new wife told the principal of my elementary school that they had a court order saying that neither me nor my mother were allowed to talk to my little brother and sister on school property. They also threatened to take them out of school if they didn't comply. The school could have gotten sued for that since they only took their word. There weren't any legal documents presented because there weren't any legal documents stating that was the case. That lie ended up doing me damage. I'll never forget the day a teacher I trusted broke my heart.

Sometime after their lie to the school, as I was walking to the "bus porch" to wait on my mom to pick me up one afternoon, I noticed my little brother waiting on the steps, too. I didn't know about the so-called court order at the time.

My brother looked so pitiful because he had been crying from being taken away from his mother. Every night he would cry and have to take medicine for his upset stomach. He was a constant wreck and he was only seven years old. So I headed to sit with my baby brother and console him. That's what I did during the fights, and that is what I was going to do then.

On my way to cheer him up, a teacher stopped me dead in my tracks and told me I wasn't allowed to talk to him on school grounds. Not only did they make my mother an outcast with their rumors of lies as well as some truth, their deliberate actions to intentionally hurt her made me feel like one, too.

During the court trials, my ex-dad brought out all my mother's spiritual experiences. She didn't deny anything that was true. He was wrong for lying under oath about smoking pot and having my soon to be close friends over for parties where he gave them alcohol underage. All of my mother's demons were put out on display while he denied his. So yes, she was seen as the crazy one, he wasn't. When in actuality, they both were wounded souls, no one being in any better state to raise a child.

During this time, my new name became "outcast" and "crazy," like the entire town started calling my mother. His new wife was a cheerleading coach and teacher at the local high school and was spreading my mother's experiences to my peers while he told everyone he knew about my mother's erratic behavior. The crazy looks they gave my mother were directed at me, too. They didn't change their facial expression when they would look from her to me. I hadn't done anything to deserve everyone's rejection, but I felt it everywhere I went. And that would be why I am so sensitive to rejection to this day.

NEGLECT

When my mom would take my siblings home from their visitation with her, I originally would always ride with her. Then, the drive to take them home back to the house I once resided in ended up being too much for me to handle. I was too proud for tears and breaking down at that time in my life. That fifteen minute drive brought back so many happy memories of a time I once had a home to return to. It was too much to bear.

I quit going with her to take them back because I would rather suppress my emotions and not have to feel them than face them as an early teen. Plus, I had no one to talk to anyways. I even detached from my siblings for a period of time because they represented the divorce and what hurt me inside. It wasn't their fault, but they served as a reminder of the life I once had because they were still happily living in it and I wasn't since my mom didn't receive the house in the divorce.

When my mother lost custody of Josh and Carrie she decided to go back to court. During the seven years she fought to get them back they were her primary focus. Every time we would go to my momaw's to visit, winning Josh and Carrie back was always the topic of conversation. I was not being emotionally raised or cared for.

At this time, I became very insecure and quiet. I wouldn't let my family photograph me because I felt unattractive, and I became withdrawn from everyone. Previous to all of the drama, I was outgoing and confident. I started claiming I was an atheist to be rebellious against my mother and her God. Part of this was due to hormones, but the other part was all of the pain I was unable to process and the belief that He was to blame for it all.

DEFENSIVENESS

Over time, it seemed as if people were scared to approach me, maybe even intimidated. That is exactly the way I wanted it. I put up the unapproachable front on purpose. Now it really bothers me if I hear people are intimidated by me. I love everyone and if they are scared to approach me or talk to me, we are all missing out on knowing each other.

I never went to a counseling session until I was twenty-one years old which was a major parenting error. We all should have been in counseling after that divorce, my mother included. I remember my piano teacher, my great-aunt Ruth telling me one day during my lesson, "You know, Celia, if you ever need to talk about anything, I am here for you."

I turned my head to the right away from her direction as she spoke and I looked out her window at her magnolia tree, fighting back my tears. That is what I so badly needed to do. I needed to talk, and I needed to cry.

THE WALL

If someone came up to me when I was hurting, wrapped their genuinely loving arms around me and held me tight, depending on how bad I was hurting I might fight them at first—but not for long. I would break down as a child, and even as an adult.

My wall was the unapproachable front. It was the look I would give others that said to stay away from me even though deep down I desperately wanted someone to reach out. But if only someone were to have put their feelings of potential rejection aside and genuinely reached out, their actions would have shown that they cared enough to try to get through to me more than any words could ever convey.

The wall was actually a pretty genius way of survival that I came up with to avoid being hurt by others. That wall prevented others from having any sort of affect on me, good or bad. It was one of my defense mechanisms. I discovered it felt better not to feel the pain people would inflict upon me. They could look at me like an outcast, say things about my mother and say things about me, and I was "comfortably numb." But the only problem with the wall is that I blocked out the love, too.

Pastor Dan at New Beginnings Church broke down my wall easily several years later when I was twenty-years-old. He had such compassion on me and my situation. What if New Beginnings had another pastor at the time? I needed someone to not just smile at me; I needed someone that understood me.

Thankfully, Pastor Dan knew where I was coming from. He was able to tell me, "I promise that you will get through this, because I have." He openly talked about his former days. If he didn't tell the church about his past, I wouldn't have believed that he had any idea what I had been through. He wasn't ashamed of his past because he saw his story through God's eyes. He wasn't in denial, and he didn't try to keep it swept under a rug. I know that being real with others can help them because I know what it meant to me. Pastor Dan was transparent. And only because of his openness was he able to reach me. He helped me most by giving me hope.

MY MOM

My ex-dad and his new wife were wrong for getting laughs out of everyone alienating my mother because of their gossip. But as a child, I was more impacted than her. My mother didn't like it, but she knew God was real and that the only explanation for everyone's behavior was spiritual warfare. Plus, my mom to this day doesn't care what anyone thinks, and she isn't very social. Therefore, she didn't lose any sleep over other's opinion of her, while I was the one negatively impacted.

As soon as her and my ex-dad separated, she opened a non-denominational mission. And she remarried as fast as he did. Her new husband would be the new pastor at the mission.

The more the town talked about her for starting a mission where they served meals, ran a food drive, and even provided shelter for homeless people, the more it added to her fire for God. The more she was attacked and persecuted she felt solely for righteousness sake like it talks about in Matthew 5:10, the more she knew she was doing the right thing. Her fire for God was only fueled by the town's attacks on her.

She renamed the mission several times, but one of the names caused a lot of controversy. One of the names of the mission was "Blood-n-Fire," which did not help matters for our small-minded, small town.

Blood-n-Fire was a Christian non-denominational church/organization in Atlanta that her new husband had visited. The organization said my new step-dad and my mother's mission could be affiliated and title their mission with the same name.

Their sign was exactly like the one in Atlanta, but it caused some major controversy. The words on the sign looked like they were written in blood, and it had a black background; this all only added to the notion that my mom was "crazy" because no one used their God-given analytical skills to research the organization.

With all the rumors going around about her sacrificing animals at the mission, a title of "Blood -n- Fire" only added to the town's fear and thoughts of her being insane. But trust me, no chickens or any other animals were ever sacrificed, although there was plenty of speaking in tongues and throwing up demons in trash cans. And if that was something that makes my family uncomfortable me mentioning, then they should have taken after me and sheltered me from their behavior as a little girl which they did not.

ANOTHER BRIGHT SIDE

Another bright side, feeling like an outcast and crazy like my mother at twelve prepared me for my future ministry, whatever He wants that to entail. It especially prepared me for the potential talk that could surround me writing my story out in book form. Although I admit I am worried what people will think as far as my good girl image going out the window, persecution for things of spiritual nature doesn't scare me.

I have an army of angels and the almighty God as my protection. I have the brain of a twenty-five-year-old woman, so I know how to process events. And if I need help processing them, which I may from time to time, I now know where to go. I am not a deceived little twelve-year-old girl anymore. Bring on the "spiritual warfare."

SPIRITUAL WARFARE

Spiritual warfare is exactly what is going on when people hurt you, your children, or your other family members for no good reason. When someone is attacked from all angles possible only after they begin pressing in to God, it is because they are obviously a threat to Satan.

Do people typically persecute and give evil glares to the mentally ill when they are not harming anyone? My mom wasn't using drugs or sacrificing animals. She was running a homeless shelter, and she was being delivered from demons. Not many people understand deliverance, and if anyone gets that, it is me.

But please explain to me how someone in their right mind could think she and her daughter would be worthy of everyone's look of disgust. Compassion? Absolutely. If you are looking at someone in disgust who is going through hard times, you are representing evil at its finest. There is no other way to put it. Ultimately I detached from her, and I joined along with those that treated her like she was crazy because I could not take the persecution any longer. That just means I was evil, too.

See, if the situation were to occur now, I could handle it because I would see right through what was going on like she did. I have received many apologies from people in the small town I grew up in who played their part before they were saved. They don't approach my mother with their apologies out of guilt and embarrassment, I assume, but they confide in me, and I pass the message along.

Their words are all the same, "I am so sorry. Now I know your mother was never crazy." I love them and I forgive them, and it is in the past. I don't hold it against them, but their apologies have meant more to me than I could ever express. I am thankful that God led them to apologize because it touched a part of my heart that needed healing. Apologies go a long way in this heart of mine.

No, that small town wasn't the world. But as a child who hasn't seen much of the world, what could be worse? Being made fun of as an adult? I don't think so. How about a guy not liking me because his parents told him that my mom "threw up demons in a trash can" when I was thirteen-years-old? Nothing could have topped that at the time.

From an adult perspective, that was her personal business that her ex-husband should have kept private, out of respect. God doesn't see that situation as anything less than wrong, and the only qualms He would have with me stating that fact is if it were from an unhealed perspective, it was untrue, or if my heart was still bitter. Bitterness is not in this heart anymore.

BLAMED GOD

I didn't initially turn my back on God when the persecution was going on. But when my mother and God's craziness uprooted me from a house I grew up in—where all my trophies, report cards, and story writing contests I had won in school stayed and I was moved away from my little brother and sister—a cloud of darkness came over me so thick, I was ready to go to heaven. I prayed Jesus would just hurry up and come back. Eventually, the resentment set in for both my mother and God. I believed Satan's whispering lies that God was the reason for all the havoc and pain and that He was enjoying seeing me suffer.

During church services, my mother forced me to go up to the front and have others lay their hands on my head to receive prayer often; it was wrong and she knows that now. Although I would have loved to get her thrown in jail for child abuse for forcing me to do anything against my will back then, making your child receive prayer just isn't against the law. And her belief in the power of prayer just might have kept me alive in the years to follow.

A lot of the times I was made to receive prayer was at this country, spirit-filled church during their nightly revival that I was made to attend with her. This revival lasted months. We were always going to church every night of the week. It wasn't a balanced way of living. And I hated every minute of it.

She couldn't make her husband or my other siblings go to church every night of the week, but she could make me. There was a lot of deliverance going on. I saw demons cast out of people, and I saw them manifest in crazy ways because they like to "show out" when there is an audience.

I saw blood vessels popping out of more than one family member's face and neck while being restrained as they kicked, roared and screamed before one of their demons finally left. I witnessed my mother throwing up demons in trash cans constantly, not just at church. Maybe if I had grown up seeing all of this it wouldn't have scared me as much. But at twelve, when all I had ever known was, "Read verse one and four out of your hymnal," sit, listen, sing another hymn, then be dismissed from your church service, it was traumatic. I developed a fear of demons, and that is exactly what Satan would rather us do if we believe in their existence at all: be afraid.

While receiving prayer at the country church one night at twelve years old, as I sat with my head down so mad at God, I told Him to "Go away" in my heart as mean, true, and as heartfelt as I possibly could. I was wearing a pink, ribbed mock turtleneck sweater as I stared down at the seat of the cream-colored pew. I meant it with all of my heart; although I had no idea where turning my back on God would lead my life.

By this time, I truly believed He was to blame for it all. He was the one driving my mother to go to church every day, and He was the one driving her to become obsessed with Him. For years I felt if only my mother hadn't went to that stupid Benny Hinn concert and got filled with the Holy Spirit, my life would still be "normal."

LACK OF BALANCE AND STABILITY

It wasn't God or the Holy Spirit driving my mother. I believe Satan is behind obsessions. I believe if he can't beat a child of God, he will weasel his way in to try to mess with them somehow.

Whereas Satan is behind obsessions, erratic behavior and instability, God is all about peace. I think of God as having a chilled out personality; He just wants us to spend time with Him and do what is in our best interest, so He gives us His commandments and His principles to live by. If we crave excitement, He can fulfill that need. But He doesn't expect us to go to church every night of the week. What I was seeing that was being told to me was God wasn't always true. Therefore, I was deceived into blaming the wrong one.

My mom simply lost her balance for a while. She was a fanatic. She experienced Him in a very powerful way one night that changed her life. She went from being an empty woman craving validation to feeling completely filled and loved in one night. I can relate to her now that I have had my own experiences with Him.

The thing is you always have to maintain a proper perspective about things. You shouldn't lose your head when it comes to falling in love with someone, even when it comes to falling in love with God. You can't be so heavenly minded that you're of no earthly good. You have to stay grounded and stable.

Immediately following the divorce, we moved houses several times in a few short years, and I was allowed to change schools throughout high school quite a bit. The first place we moved into after being kicked out of our house with the in ground pool, the home where all my clothes and trophies stayed, was into a basement in downtown South Pittsburg, where there was no sunlight seeping through windows.

The lack of sunlight encouraged me to sleep more than usual. Sleeping too much was a perfect opportunity to feed my depression. My depression was written all over my face in pictures from that time in my life. Although I was depressed, it wasn't until the summer I was fifteen that the downward spiral began. That God-awful downward spiral lasted five years and took me five more years to fully recover.

DEALING WITH THE BITTER PARTS

My heart hurts for those whose childhood innocence was robbed in a more severe way than mine, such as specifically from abuse, sexual and/or physical. If I were in their shoes, I would need to hear that it wasn't my fault and that it doesn't make me defective. The little girl or boy inside of those who have been abused has a voice. And that's why I am a firm believer that writing out what their abusers did to them, however painful it may be, helps.

Although I am not bitter or resentful now, there were parts of my heart that were for a while. No counselor or friend could ever change what happened or take it away. The town turned against me.

I felt like my mother was crazy and God made her that way. The teachers I loved didn't seem to love me as much anymore, and my ex-dad abandoned me all in one season. And the hardest part of all is forgiving someone who doesn't even seem sorry for hurting you, let alone express it.

But God showed me how the very things that were done to me, I have done to others in some way at some point in time. I have made someone feel rejected and left out. I have hurt others' hearts, too. And I know I wouldn't want someone being bitter toward me for my past wrongdoings.

"So in everything, do to others what you would have them do to you, for this sums up the Law and the Prophets" (Matthew 7:12, NIV).

I have been hurt and I have done the hurting. The truth is the people who hurt me either did it on purpose or they were deceived. Either way, He doesn't love me any more than He loves those that hurt me. I have been misled before. Everyone deserves forgiveness.

I have my voice and it has a right to be heard. But what about the others out there who I hurt?

My own self-awareness provides me with understanding toward those who have hurt me. That awareness helped heal my heart and I hope it inspires you to do the same if you can at all relate.

HATE

Bitterness is a close relative of hatred. And I never thought I could hate anyone. I thought I was above hatred. I was too sweet of a person to hate anyone. But how sweet is bitter?

When God brought to attention the bitterness in my heart, I asked Him to remove that and any hate in my heart for the people who hurt me without remorse and replace it with His love. Guess what I discovered when I asked Him to do that?

At first, I couldn't put my finger on why I was getting overly emotional about it. Then, I realized it was because I was feeling ashamed. The only Father I will ever be really close to in the way I desire and the One who healed my broken heart was disappointed in me for letting hate in.

And that is why I cast bitterness and hatred far from me. I prayed to be free from them and never be tempted to allow those sinful feelings back in my heart, no matter what happens and who hurts me in the future. It was something inside of me that didn't make Him proud. Bitterness is ugly, and when it shows on the outside, so am I.

HE NEVER LEFT MY SIDE

Through my younger childhood days, I was secretly convinced that I was His favorite. I swear He told my heart that once. And no worries, He is big enough to make us each individually feel that way. Good thing I have learned how to share since then, too.

I wrote the poem below when I was eight years old. I was in Knoxville, Tennessee, with my momaw, visiting her mother and sister. I was sitting in the sunlit den by the window when I wrote it. My grandparents put it in the newspaper and had it framed shortly thereafter. My popaw, John Swafford, is retired but still a Southern Baptist preacher. Needless to say, they were proud of their little granddaughter.

Although my personality has always been that of a wild child, my heart wants to love God more than any other child of His. I want His favor and all the blessings He wants to give me. My desire to love Him and be a good girl never left even when I strayed. He has always been the better part of me. I was and always will be His.

God is Everything

God is lord,
God is king,
God is everything,
God is some one you can count on,
And God can make your problems go away,
Just in a flash of day,
So if you want that to happen I would pray,
Oh dear God help me solve my problems,
Please oh please right away.

A=men

Saturday, February 5, 1994

By: Celia Marie Anzalone Hill

FEELING LOST? SO WAS I

For the uncontrolled, there is no wisdom. For the uncontrolled there is no concentration, and for him without concentration, there is no peace. And for the unpeaceful how can there ever be happiness?

Anonymous

MALE ATTENTION

I started to realize that something wasn't right with me besides depression when I was working at my mom's furniture store in the summer of 2000. It had been two years since my mom and ex-dad divorced. This older man whom I had known since I was seven years old started paying special attention to me. What happened between us is one of my most embarrassing and most ashamed of stories. And it was only the beginning of the very dark years.

That whole situation was the first time I felt the power trip feeling that came along from receiving male attention. When he would ask me to pull my skirt up higher, I felt gross inside. And although I would tell him no, that didn't stop me from wearing the short skirts and making sure to walk by him in hopes to receive his compliments, even though they were dirty. And that didn't stop me from pretending to be ok with his advances. He was meeting a need inside me that longed specifically for male attention, good or bad.

I enjoyed the attention all the while knowing it was wrong. Every day I would come home and record what was going on in my diary. I wrote about how guilty I felt but that I couldn't stop it and was unsure of where it was going. I remember him telling me not to put anything he said to me in my diary at fifteen years old. Poor guy should have known better than that. I had to tell someone.

All of the talk and teasing finally led up to an afternoon where he had one of my mom's other employees watch the warehouse entrance. Then, he begged me to come back to the warehouse with him as a small child would beg to get his way with a parent. While there, he kissed me and touched me briefly and inappropriately. Less than three seconds into it, I jerked away and breezed past the other man watching guard to the safety which I found all alone in the bathroom in the front of the 30,000 sq foot building.

I ran straight to the bathroom to cry, but the tears didn't surface. I thought I was going to get sick, but I never did. I knew better; I had a conscience, and he was old for my age. I wasn't physically attracted to him at all. And nothing like that ever happened again because I immediately quit working for my mother after that in order to avoid him altogether.

MODESTY

I was the most transparent I have ever been when I was at my worst. That is the only thing I envy about who I was in the past. I didn't care what anyone thought of me. And that was obvious.

Although I admire that mindset, I am ashamed that I wasn't concerned with how I could have been affecting others in a negative way. Sin begins in the heart. You can sin with your thoughts even if you aren't acting them out.

But even though I was wrong for dressing immodestly years ago, I feel that that some of the women who claimed to be lovers of Christ and even wives of pastors were equally wrong for giving me hateful looks from their disapproval. God has grace because He understands our insecurities, but do you think God is pleased with judging any more than He is with immodesty?

"Do not judge so that you will not be judged" (Matthew 7:1, NAS).

I have seen and experienced both views and ways of the world. Everyone wants to be my friend and send smiles and compliments my way when I am where I should be according to their eyes. But the people I respect the most are the ones that have never treated me any differently; no matter what phase of my life, regardless of how I was dressing or acting out, they have treated me the same.

I pray for your heart's condition to be revealed to you right now and that God would bring you to repentance if you don't see the sin in judging a girl for how she dresses. Spend time in the presence of your Lord, and your heart will see that she is seeking out attention from a place of confusion. Good or bad attention is still attention. She doesn't really want your man if you're a female and you have one. In fact, if she is anything like I was, she wouldn't even know how to feel comfortable being truly loved by a man.

Even now, I don't want to let anyone in, not in the real way, at least not for awhile.

I don't want anyone seeing me in this state of brokenness in the process of repair. People are only allowed in as deep as the parts of me I deem acceptable. It would be too much for people to see how deep my pain is at this time in person. But as time goes on and I continue to heal, I will let people inside fully, inside the real way.

And the females out there who are being judged like I was, I am sure they are the same way. I try to keep a perspective Jesus would be proud of when it comes to my view of others whom I don't understand. How do I know what someone's childhood was like unless they tell me? And until they do, I won't ever know what led them to the place I find fault-worthy. So I never treat someone differently for their appearance or actions. I have my own experience with feeling misunderstood to thank for that.

Thoughtfulness for others, generosity, modesty, and self-respect are the qualities which make a real gentleman or lady.
Thomas Huxley

CUTTING

When I was ten years old, one of my friends said that she wanted to be a prostitute after we watched *Milk Money* with Melanie Griffith. At ten, I still had a properly functioning brain, so I thought something was seriously wrong with her. But little did I know that one day the idea to cut myself would originate from a movie I would see on television.

Television and movies also made parties and cocaine attractive to me. Any time I saw someone snort a line of cocaine from a mirror on a movie, I very rarely saw them having any other experience less than enjoyable. Needless to say, I won't take my child's viewing pleasure lightly if I ever have one.

Within a few months after I quit working for my mother, I began cutting my left forearm out of curiosity. I wanted to be a cutter so I could receive some sort of release from the pain I felt, but I couldn't ever be a successful "cutter" since it wasn't in me to go too deep. I couldn't take much physical pain in that form. I always wanted my mom to notice the nicks so there was some attention seeking going on behind that behavior as well. During this time,

I also began going to parties, smoking pot on the weekends, and sneaking out with my friends regularly.

BEING SNEAKY

When three of my friends and I were sneaking back in through my window at five in the morning after a night of partying, as the last one of us were sneaking back in she bumped into my entertainment center causing the candle resting on top of it to tumble down to the ground creating a loud thump. As we were racing to jump back into my bed, we could hear my mom coming down the stairs. She came to check on us because she heard the noise. When she asked what had happened, I told her that it was just one of my friends trying to show us her gymnastics moves. My mom believed us and went back to bed.

Within a month from that sneaking-out incident, two of my girlfriends and I skipped the first block of school. We would've skipped all day if we could find someone to pick us up and take us somewhere to drink alcohol. As we were aimlessly walking around the neighborhood, someone called the school and told on us. The lack of trouble to get into along with finding out we were busted led us back to school before lunchtime. When we got there, we tried to play it off as if we were going in late. But my mom, surprisingly, didn't buy it that time.

RUNAWAY TRAIN WRECK: PART ONE

When my mom told me she was taking me out of the public school as punishment, I decided to run away for the first time. I brought one of my girlfriends with me and I wasn't very successful. I even went to my ex-dad's on my way to wherever my crazy mind thought I was going to go and left a letter to him in his mailbox.

My friend and I ended up staying at one of her older friend's house that night. The following day, I sat around at her friend's house by myself while my friend went to school like normal. I had no game plan at all on how I was going to stay away from my mother forever. And it wasn't long until my mom was contacting the school and my friends to find out where I was.

By mid-afternoon my friend called to tell me my mom was on the way and that the cops had road blocks set up to stop me. The school threatened her that if she didn't tell my mother where I was she wouldn't be allowed to be in homecoming court.

My mom ended up pressing charges against my friend's older friend. To this day, the woman seems to not take responsibility for her actions of housing a young runaway. She spent a night in jail but my punishment was worse. I had to go back home and face my mother.

She got very strict and turned up the control when I came back home. Then one evening a few days later, I snapped during a fight. I don't remember what the fight was about, but when I snapped I do remember acting the craziest I have ever acted sober.

That night after I got out of the shower, I cut my wrist to scare my mom with no intentions of killing myself, but it was still deeper than usual. And it was even with a knife instead of a small razor. It was official; I was losing my mind.

INPATIENT STAY

When I was taken to a behavior health facility where I stayed for three days, I made a countdown of the days I had left until I was eighteen. I don't remember the days, but it was over two-and-a-half years away. That was pretty depressing.

The psychiatrist who evaluated me at the hospital said that I didn't need any medication. He said I had a behavioral problem. He drew a dot on a piece of paper with another dot on the opposite side. He said my way of getting to that other dot was by creating circles. He said the cutting was for attention, which I already knew. He also said, "This too shall pass," and that I needed to live with my dad.

Personally, I agree with the psychiatrist, I didn't need medication and I am thankful they didn't give me any. Medication may have made me numb and masked my craziness, but it wouldn't have taken away the underlying issue that was causing me to misbehave.

If they had medicated me, I would have never had to deal with the root (spiritual) issue because I would've never had to cry "help" to God when I finally hit rock bottom. I am a firm believer that rock bottoms can either kill you or make you stronger. They can either make you or break you. After all, when you reach the bottom, the only other direction you can go is up.

THE DIARY

While I was at the behavior health facility for the night I snapped and cut myself where my mother could see, my mom and my aunt read my infamous diary. I never heard the end of that from my friends. They all said if I just hadn't written in the diary, everything wouldn't have come out. Before my mom read my diary, all she knew is that I skipped first block of school and I was acting nutty.

When my mom and my aunt Amy read it, they highlighted the bad parts and everything. When I got it back, the yellow highlighting bled through the pages. Then my mom became her version of protective by disconnecting the cable, phone lines, taking me out of school completely, and by keeping a constant watch over me when she could and for the times she couldn't, she hired a babysitter who was only one year older than me and who went to the Christian private home school academy my mother was planning to send me to.

It made me feel crazy. The babysitter looked at me like she was better and I looked at her like I was better. She was a square and had been homeschooled practically her whole life. What did she know about having lots of friends and being popular? What did she know about having the kind of fun I was getting involved in? Years down the road, I became friends with this person. But even now, I struggle with resenting her being on my mother's side during that time of imprisonment it felt like.

I was no longer being treated like a normal child. It was a form of child abuse to take a child out of school and reduce her contact to no one but yourself. My friends would have to park past my house just to sneak me notes when I would be outside swinging on the porch. That was my only form of recreation for over three weeks straight other than walking with my mother every morning at five.

But there was truly a lot going on that would freak a parent out, right? Imagine you are in her shoes. You open your daughter's diary and read an older guy you had been employing for years was constantly coming on to her, turn the page to discover she had been drinking at parties and sneaking out of her window at night. You think, *No wonder they were always playing "dress up" before "bed."*

RUNAWAY: TAKE TWO

My mother is a control freak to this day, and I was a little terror of a daughter when I didn't get my way. And after being on lockdown for over three weeks, I had to get out. I forgive her now just like she forgives me for leaving the shower running while I "escaped."

I packed my things in a pillowcase before church and hid my things in my old room. That room quickly became my brother's room after she knew I could sneak out of it. My new room was on the second floor. But what she didn't know is that one day I would successfully manage to sneak out of that one, too.

I stuffed my pillowcase with the essentials: toothpaste, toothbrush, my diary, pen, some makeup, and her spare key to the car. I bought two packs of cigarettes on the way and, thankfully, had a full tank of gas, because I didn't have any money. Where was I headed? I had no idea. I only knew I wanted out.

When I was driving, heading to my unknown destination, I knew I was being crazy. I knew what was going on wasn't normal. But I had to get away from her, as bad as it sounds. We were clashing. Even to this day, if I feel like someone is trying to control me, I get out quick. I hate the feeling because I like to be in control of own my environment and my life.

After about four hours of driving, I got sleepy. I thought I could just park my car at a rest area and sleep in it, but I wasn't sure if that was legal and didn't want to risk getting caught, so I stopped at a Waffle House to find someone who looked safe enough to ask if I could park my car at a rest area without any issues. I ordered a black coffee that I didn't even drink. I didn't sit there for long before I spotted my guy.

When I asked him if I could park my car at a rest area, he said he had a better place in mind—his garage.

We talked in his garage all night. I sat in my car while he stood by one of his cars. We concocted this plan where I could hide out until I turned eighteen and work in Gatlinburg at one of his friend's shops while getting paid under the table.

What an awesome plan! I was thinking. I would never have to deal with my parents again. That night, I wrote in my diary about the good news while parked in his garage, up the hill from his house. The next day he talked to a friend of his about our plan and came home with news. The friend was a cop and told him he could get in trouble for harboring a "runaway" who had an "APB" out for her arrest. That just meant I had to come up with another plan, because I wasn't going home.

I went to his town's local library and got directions to my dad's house in Pennsylvania. After that, I followed the nice man to the gas station. He put gas in my car and pumped it for me because I didn't know how to pump gas yet, and I didn't have any money. He left me with his number and told me to call when I was safe. I never did call because I lost his number, although I still remember the nice man's name to this day. It was Charlie.

Hours down the road, I finally called my dad and told him what I was doing. He already knew I had run away from talking to my mom, so he went ballistic. He told me to turn around, and he'd fly me up instead. But no way was I going back home after stealing my mom's car. So I drove and drove, and didn't get caught. Finally, I got to where I was only three hours from my dad's. I called my dad, and he said get to a hotel and that he would come get me.

He gave the hotel I checked into his credit card number and told me, "Stay inside, do not leave. We will be right there to get you."

All I had eaten that day was a hot dog at the nice man from the Waffle House's home. I also drank a beer out of a can with his dad while he was at work. His dad was cool, and he had no idea I was only fifteen. He was also oblivious to the fact that I was a girl on the run. I guess he believed his son when he told him he picked me up at the Waffle House. After all, it was the truth—only the other way around.

As soon as I checked in my hotel in Harrisonburg, Virginia, I looked out my window and saw that there was a Waffle House across the street. So I ignored my dad's command to stay in my room because I was just going to drive across the street to eat. After all, how much trouble could possibly ensue from that?

When I started to pull out, I saw a cop car parked at the Waffle House, and it made me nervous. That must have been the reason why I took an immediate left rather going past the median in the road to the side where the cars taking a left from my position would go. I took a left toward what could have been ongoing traffic.

BUSTED

The cops said that they were impressed I made it that far. They also said they thought I was drunk at first for taking that left. After talking to my dad, they didn't arrest me in handcuffs or anything. I've actually never been put it handcuffs to this day, but I have been to three different police stations under the age of eighteen.

When they first pulled me over, one of the cops searched my purse and found two packs of cigarettes. He didn't take them away, but he did tell my dad as we were leaving, "Oh and by the way, your daughter has cigarettes." I didn't shoot the cop a mean look. I only looked back and smiled because I was two steps ahead of him. He should've been more specific and told my dad I had two packs of cigarettes like he knew I did. When my dad was appropriately going off on me, he demanded I hand him my "pack of cigarettes."

"Sure thing, Dad" was my response as I handed them over from the backseat still left with an unopened pack.

OPPRESSION AND HIS PROTECTION

What was the inner drive to hurt myself and escape reality about? Can we agree that was not normal? Experiencing pain is one thing, but what I was going through was quite another.

I believe when I told God to go away I opened up a door for Satan to oppress me without God intervening on my behalf. Although I could never be possessed by Satan since I've never once given my soul away, he is always capable of oppressing us. The more I had my back turned on God, the more subject I was to being attacked by demonic infestation. And yes, even Christians can have their share of demons.

But the advantages to being a Christian in the demonic realm is that when I realize I am being attacked now, by faith I know I can say, for instance, "Spirit of fear, you have no authority to attack me. I renounce whatever I have watched or done to invite you in. I rebuke you and command you to flee from me and my house in Jesus' name." It works.

It doesn't mean Satan's demons will leave me alone for good, but I always have control of the moment when I bring up Jesus' name. In my experience, just mentioning the blood of Jesus in the presence of demonic forces does to them what light does to vampires in movies. I know it sounds cliché, but it is the only way I know how to describe it.

GOD'S MERCY

Anytime I have ever prayed and fasted for something, my prayers are either answered or He reveals His perspective and truth regarding the situation. As soon as I asked God to help me when I met my first pit, things immediately began to turn around for me. He didn't hesitate to rescue me when I called on Him for help, and He wouldn't for anyone else either.

Although He wasn't going to protect me from Satan's attacks because I told Him to go away and I wasn't asking for His protection those years I went down the wrong path, I do believe He kept me from death all the times I totaled my cars without injury. The times I interacted on a personal level with strangers, I remained safe. My drug overdoses never turned deadly, and my record is spotless when I should be serving overlapping sentences.

I believe when my mother prayed that He would close my womb until it was His will, He answered a mother's prayer for her daughter. One out of three or four sexually active people will contract a sexually transmitted disease in their lifetime, and I never once contracted any diseases from my promiscuity. I can't deny His hand on my life. His love had to have been what covered me.

"Above all, keep your love for one another at full strength, since love covers a multitude of sins" (1 Peter 4:8, CSB).

He listens to all of our prayers, but it's not His nature to force Himself on anyone. He will pursue, but He won't smother or try to force anyone to love Him back. He's a gentleman. You tell Him to go, and He backs off. He wanted communion with Him to be my decision. That would be the beauty of free will He has given me.

Runaway train never comin' back. Runaway train tearin' up the track. Runaway train burnin' in my veins. Run away but it always seems the same..

Partial lyrics to "Runaway Train" by Tom Petty and the Heartbreakers

LOVE AND OTHER DRUGS

Celia, do you want to know what I think? I think you should become a nun.

> My dad after reading my "Dear God" poem

FIRST LOVE

The last completely healthy relationship I have been in was when I was ten years old. I had a crush on that boy for over a year before he liked me back. During my crush season, he called me the bubble queen to make fun of me when we were on the swing set. I grew up allergic to mosquito bites and I would always scratch them, which probably caused the infected bubbles. My mom would have to pop them with a needle and medicate my bites with pink calamine lotion throughout the spring and summertime. I would come to school with pink all over me. It was so gross, and he had obviously noticed.

And even though he told everyone I cried when one of my favorite teachers moved schools, I still liked him and would write God letters asking Him to bring us together. Then one day in the middle of one of our letters, he called me and asked me to be his girlfriend. God often answers this girl's prayers.

He was my boyfriend for four months until I felt smothered. That length of time at ten-years-old felt like an eternity. I noticed I was sick of him when we were sitting on the couch and he had his arms around me. He always would have his arms around me before, but this time it felt different. It felt like he was hanging all over me. All I wanted to do was play with my friends at a birthday party rather than act like a couple on the couch.

He got his feelings hurt that I was getting tired of him. It made me feel sick when I saw him sad because I was ignoring him at another birthday party; this time it was mine. I felt bad for hurting him, but I didn't know how to handle the situation. My mom even got on to me about it. But rather than break up with him, I found it easier to purposefully ignore him into breaking up with me.

I knew how much I liked him and how I wanted to be with him for a whole year before he liked me back, and it worried me that the feeling didn't last like I thought it would.

I asked God if I was always going to be that way. I already had concerns if marriage was going to be in the cards for me at ten years old. So by the time I saw *Sister Act* at eleven, I decided I wanted to be a nun. The sisters had so much fun together in that movie, even when they were doing yard work.

THE UNHEALTHY ONES

Fast-forward to the crazy years; the only relationships I knew were unhealthy and codependent. And those relationships brought out the very worst in me. Yes, they were wrong for verbally and physically abusing me. But I was wrong for using them to determine my own identity and worth.

And I learned how to fight with words just as well.

I would give them what I called love with expectations of getting this so called love in return. It was never the kind of love God would have for me to share with another. I was using them and

I believe they were using me too. For that is what codependency looks like. But I will never truly know their hearts like God does.

I REMEMBER YOU, DO YOU REMEMBER ME TOO?

My first serious boyfriend and I started dating when I was seventeen years old, it was in November of 2002. Take away all the sin, and the truth is there was something there. I had a crush on him since I was little, in fact all the girls did. He was the older brother of a girl I grew up with in our small town. I'll call him Hunter.

I got a guy that was a challenge, not the easy guys that any girl can have, but the kind that when they choose you, inside you feel special. He was twenty-one and he had his pick, and he chose me. That told me I was worth something instead of nothing.

Hunter and I would spend time together every day. He made me feel protected and safe the first few months. And that was something I felt was missing in my life, a male's protection due to not having a father figure.

We would ride around and get high every day. One of the first times we hung out before we started dating, I did cocaine for the third time. But when we got serious, he didn't want either of us to have any part of it. Looking back, I can understand why. He had been doing cocaine longer than I had and knew it was evil. At first, there aren't any horrible coming down experiences. There are only good times. But, he knew something that I didn't. I started dating him in October of 2002, and I didn't do coke again until my eighteenth birthday in April of 2003.

When I got a job waitressing in January of 2003, it caused a fight because it would take away from time we could spend together. He worked a full-time job during the day, and I would be working nights. We were always together before I got a job. For the first part of our relationship, he was my only friend and the only person I confided in. We were both jealous of anyone else even being close to us. If we could've had it our way, it would have just been us in our own little world.

ANY FORM OF ABUSE IS NOT "OKAY"

The first time I knew I should leave him was during a fight. He had come to my work and had eaten in the section I was serving. Apparently he had overheard these boys talking about me to their server. The server was overheard by my boyfriend saying, "Yeah, she's pretty, but she's a bit dingy."

Then my boyfriend said in my defense, "Hey, you might want to watch who you talk about with her boyfriend sitting right behind you."

I didn't see or hear any of this, but when I went to his table to check on him, he started going off on me like I had done something wrong. He accused me of "hooking up" with said server behind his back. That server was not my type at all at the time. He was the type I considered to be a square at the time. He definitely didn't do drugs, and he was a Christian. How boring.

When I defended the server, it didn't help matters. He was causing a scene, and for the most part, I still had some class and found it embarrassing. He felt I defended him because we were involved. But the truth is I defended the server because it didn't offend me that he said that. I usually came to work stoned like the majority of my coworkers. Pot made me very dingy. I would say the silliest things when I was high. Now I know the reason why he was so bothered was because I wasn't validating his feelings, but at the time I didn't understand. At seventeen, I had no idea how to argue or be in a serious relationship. At twenty-five, count me out of the game for just a little while longer.

FIRST SCARE

After work, I went to his house per usual. The arguing continued, and it got more intense. I finally had enough and said I was leaving. He grabbed my keys from me and pushed me down to the ground and didn't stop yelling at me. That was my first time I had ever experienced anything physical like that.

As I stared at him from the ground in fear, my mind knew it wasn't good for me to be with someone that displayed that kind of rage toward me, but it was too uncomfortable to face reality. The reality, which I would at some point have to eventually deal with, was that I was even more lost and confused about everything than when I started out. Rather than leave the relationship, I continued down the path that would lead to our further destruction.

The verbal and physical abuse continued. He never punched me or threw anything at me. But I was pushed and dragged around to the point of there being bruises all over both of my arms once. And there were bruises on more than just that occasion. He was the most verbally abusive of them all at a time in my life where it affected me the most.

PASSIVE-AGGRESSIVE

I didn't even know how to speak up when my feelings would get hurt, and I didn't know how to fight. If he did something that hurt my feelings, I would internalize the event and never release it in the way I originally received it.

If he was ever flirtatious with another girl, it naturally made me very insecure. But I felt ashamed of my feelings and embarrassed rather than owning them. I never would say how I felt out loud to him. Instead of verbalizing what I was feeling when he would do something that hurt me, I would shut down. I would get him back, but he never knew why. When we would fight, I would threaten to leave because I knew that would get his attention. When I was seventeen, I was childish and passive-aggressive.

When you are attaining your sense of self-worth from a person, you are high on life when they are affirming you. But when the words become abusive, since they are your mirror, you almost grow into them.

I had not slept around before I met him. I was not any of the things he would say about me.

When he first started hurting me with words, it broke my heart. I was still a child, and the things he would say about me weren't true. But even though I knew they weren't true, I felt that he knew more about me than I did. I felt that he believed what he was saying about me, so there must be some truth to his words. Over time, I toughened up and fought back with words. I was equally hurtful in my own way. I am ashamed at the things I would say to him and thankfully had an opportunity to apologize years later.

CLOSURE

We had a phone conversation a couple of years ago where he apologized for all the things he said to me when we were together. I cried my seventeen-year-old wounded heart out during that apology at the age of twenty-three. It was from that apology that I realized I never was what he said about me, and he knew it, too. He said he was just scared of losing me. He said that he just wanted to hold me in tight and not let go, and that ultimately his plan backfired.

I said I was sorry, too. I had plenty of guy friends that I would ride around and smoke pot with at the time and not think anything about how that would make him feel. I told him I was sorry for that and the things I would say to hurt him.

His response was, "Celia, you were just young, and so was I."

I told him the drugs took everything away from us, as a couple and individually. And that he should hate them and not touch them ever again for that reason alone. That was our last conversation, nearly three years ago. I pray right now that God will pursue and ultimately restore him, too.

MARIJUANA AND RUMORS

I smoked pot for the first time when I was thirteen to fake being cool. It wasn't until my second or third time smoking it that I realized pot and weed were the same thing. I knew I had been smoking pot because that is what my friends called it.

But when a spring break visit to my mother turned into me refusing to go back to my dad's, I began smoking pot every day with my friends. When I came back from my dad's right before my sixteenth birthday, she gave me the car I stole when I ran away. I had an 8:00 p.m. curfew during the week and a 10:00 p.m. curfew on the weekends. When I got my first report card of the semester with straight A's, which I always maintained, she upped it up to 8:30 p.m. and 10:30 p.m. All of my friends could stay out later than that, but I still managed to fit as much trouble as I could within those hours.

At sixteen-years-old, I began outwardly rebelling against people's opinion of me. During this time of my life, I would purposefully act out. The more people would talk, the funnier I thought it was. At first I cared to the point of tears, and now I viewed their nonstop gossip as my entertainment.

The truth is no one really knew what I was doing. When I was eighteen, I had a friend tell me with concern that she heard that I always had coke on me. I told her that it wasn't the truth but I wished it was.

They always said I was dating black guys because they would see me hanging out with them, and I didn't care to make new friends so the talk would stop. I would ride around with them in broad daylight in our small-minded, small town without conviction.

I have never cared what color a person is; if they treat me well, I am open to friendship. But in the small town I grew up in, being seen with those outside of your race is considered trashy and even an actual sin against God to some. I went out with this one guy who gave a scripture reference to back that view up. The scripture was taken out of context; it had nothing to do with dating outside of your race.

My mom never had a problem with me hanging out with people outside of my race. I always knew that my mom didn't care either way, which is probably why I never rebelled in that way. The only time she cared is when she found out one of my friends was a known drug dealer.

She didn't care about him being black; she cared that she heard he would get white girls hooked on drugs only to use and abuse them. I can honestly say I never saw that side of the guy I am referring to. We were never more than friends, but he made his crush clear. He may have even led people to believe we were more than friends. I didn't care what he said to people. All I cared about was getting high. And that we did, nearly every day until he went to jail.

That friendship was a major source of conflict with Hunter. When we first started dating, the old friend was in jail, but he would write me letters that I am not sure I ever even responded to. I would let my boyfriend read them, but he never believed me that we didn't do anything more than hang out because of the rumors he heard. And when someone doesn't trust me when I know I never lie, it hurts—especially coming from someone who says they love me.

Right before my eighteenth birthday, he started going off on me in front of one of his friends who swore he saw the black drug dealer and I kiss once, and I eventually hung up on him. It wasn't true, and he was supposed to be on my side.

THE DEVIL

The first line of cocaine I ever did at seventeen years old lasted hours. I didn't need more than one line, and I didn't feel bad when I came down. But over time, it took more to reach a high.

On my eighteenth birthday, I bought my first gram of cocaine without Hunter's permission. The first time I tried it six months prior, I fell in love with it. Since he didn't want us doing it anymore, I didn't, until things began going south. I had finally had it with the things he would say about me. I first rebelled against my parents, and then I started rebelling against him.

A lot of people call cocaine "the devil," which is not too far from the truth. The first time I bought it, I paid the highest one would have to pay for a gram. A few months later I was approached by someone who heard to come to me to buy larger amounts of pot. Over time, I also began selling this person coke as well.

Life during that time was about me and my best friend, cocaine. No one and nothing else mattered, and it showed. I did cocaine a few times a week on average from April 14, 2003, my eighteenth birthday, until June of 2005.

I was doing an average of two grams by myself each time I did coke after the first year of my addiction. At that time, I would hit it and the high would barely even register, let alone last more than a few minutes. What started as my first line of cocaine that lasted hours upon hours of this amazing high turned into a vicious back-to-back compulsion to take more and more, and not reach any sort of high that satisfied. But even an unsatisfied high was better than my sober reality. At that point, my reality was even darker and emptier than the reality I initially starting running from at fifteen due to the heavy drug use.

When I was nineteen, I bought my first quarter ounce of coke which is seven grams. It was the most I had ever bought on my own. I was thrilled to have that much at one time. Sound pathetic? It was. And for the first part of the night, I got high in my apartment all by myself. I never felt lonely when I did coke, and I never cried.

At some point, I decided to leave my apartment and go visit some friends. On the way, I noticed that my vision became blurred to where I couldn't recognize the numbers on my cell phone. I started to feel nauseous from the amount of cocaine I had done and threw up. Then, I did some more cocaine before having to throw up again. It was a vicious cycle of back to back key bumps and constantly throwing up green vile.

At some point during the ride in my car to visit my friends I became convinced there was someone following me. I held my key full of powder resting on top over my bag of cocaine in case I accidentally spilled it as I drove down the road in a hunched up position. I was waiting for a safe opportunity to take my next hit of cocaine which never happened in the messed up, delusional state I was in.

It was true that there was a car behind me but they weren't following me because they knew I was doing drugs. They were just behind me on the road. I felt paralyzed. My body was craving more, but I couldn't move to take it. I was tense, and my body was beginning to ache. Driving was a challenge but I finally made it to my friend's house after 40 painful minutes of being without cocaine.

I can still remember how excruciating the times between my hits of cocaine were. It brings me to tears to this day because of how blessed I feel to have made it out alive from that addiction. It wouldn't let me leave and when I started it wouldn't let me stop. It was the only time I felt peace and it didn't last long before I needed more.

When I knocked on my friend's door, I still had the bag, the key, and my shoulders in the same hunched-up position I did while I was driving. My friend opened the door and just shook his head in disappointment as he let me in.

That night, I got sick more than usual. I was used to doing coke, getting sick and doing more. I was used to throwing up green vile because there was nothing in my stomach. Getting sick was the norm for me because it made me feel better enough to where I could do more. I finally found a medicine that hit the spot and successfully distracted me from reality.

What is scary is that my initial plan with the seven grams was to do only one gram by myself and make money off the rest. But by the time I ended up weighing it at a friend's house, it was at 3.5 grams. I only had one friend stop by to see me that night, and he only did two small lines. That means I did over three grams by myself. I did the equivalent of forty-five lines that night.

To some people speedballing means one thing, but to me it was the way I felt when I smoked pot after doing some coke. That was my favorite high. Plus, it made my cocaine high last longer so I didn't have to do it as frequently if I was constantly smoking pot in between hits of cocaine.

I only took Xanax to help me go to sleep after I was finished doing coke, because they took away from my cocaine high. On more than one occasion, I was afraid I was going to die in my sleep because my heart would slow down to a very slow pace before I would fall asleep. I had one thing speeding up my heart, and the other slowing it down. I had so much speed in my system that it was not natural for my heart to be going that slow, and I knew it. My fear of dying in my sleep made me get in bed with my momaw who I was living with at the time on more than one occasion. Now, my momaw knows what that was all about.

I was in this place of being up for anything as far as drugs went. But I kept whatever bit of dignity I was trying to hold onto by never being the girl who would flash someone for more coke or do a table dance for an offered $500. But as far as drugs went, I was up for anything but crack.

MY NONNA

On another coke occasion when I was eighteen, I was doing coke in my bedroom alone. This particular night, I got the overwhelming urge to call my nonna ("grandma" in Italian). I called her and found out she had just passed away and that her funeral was that day. No one called to tell me because they felt it was my dad's responsibility. I hadn't seen my dad in three years at this time. I resented the entire situation. However, I know my Nonna, whether I was well or not, would have had me there. She unconditionally loved me. I was her pupa (doll) and bella (beauty). We always said we loved each other all the way up to the sky and down, and back and around the world a million times.

That next day, I bought more coke and drove to Florida to be with my family. When I stopped at a gas station, this man approached me to help me because I was in distress due to locking my keys in my car. He had long stringy hair and lots of missing teeth, but I wasn't scared of him. I even felt comfortable telling him how I was freaking out about my coke being in visible sight in my passenger seat. I had to find a way back in my car without calling a locksmith. After he helped me unlock my car by bending back the window so I could reach my arm inside to open the door, he offered me more drugs. He said I could follow him to do some with him.

I followed him and luckily, I wasn't murdered, taken advantage of, or hurt. He used blue food coloring with his meth, which struck me as odd. It wasn't that great at all. He even gave me some of the not-so-great blue food-colored meth to take with me. I will call him "Rickey" from now on.

When I made it to my family's house, I didn't show any form of grieving during that time, and it offended everyone. I went to her grave and didn't shed a single tear. I cry just thinking of how much I miss her now that I let myself feel.

I wasn't there during her last days because I was absorbed in myself and my lifestyle. My mom said to not be too hard on myself, all teenagers go through that. My nonna decided to give me her car some time before she passed, and I didn't even go down with my other set of grandparents to get it.

And when it was time for me to leave Florida and head home, I was so coked up that I drove four hours south down Interstate 1-75 which was the opposite direction I needed to go, by the way. I wouldn't have even realized had it not been for my mother calling to check my progress. That is in the top ten worst experiences of my life.

METH

The only reason I ever even tried meth for the first time was because there wasn't any coke around. Not many people from my past know I did meth unless they did it with me. It was my secret addiction because everyone knows how dirty it is. But you could do one line of meth and be up and going for two days. And it suppressed your appetite even more so than coke.

The only thing is, the entire high you are paranoid. And you feel like you have this icky feeling as if there are chemicals all inside your body trying to seep out from underneath your dirty-feeling skin during the high. And for days after, you feel as you have been run over by a truck with the chemicals trapped inside.

Maybe that scares you if you've never done it. I pray it does.

RICKEY REVISITED

That Rickey guy came through Chattanooga a few weeks after I met him and gave me a call. If you were going to do drugs with me for free, I would've gladly graced you with my presence. For some, just that was usually enough because of my skimpy outfits. What you wear sends a message to the world. Mine sent that I was easy, even though I never thought of myself that way. I was only after their attention and free drugs.

I guess Rickey could only take ten minutes of my chatter. He didn't try anything with me but he obviously wasn't there for friendship. As soon as he realized that talking and drugs was all I was there for, he sat a bag of meth on the table and politely said, "I will be right back." He never came back. Good call, Rickey.

WHAT GOES UP MUST COME DOWN

Coming down from cocaine was the pits. Anyone who has done it enough can tell you that coming down truly is the hardest thing. I was always the last to go to bed during the binges within my group of friends. I put off coming down as long as I could by continuing to do more. We all kept busy by playing cards for hours. I have won money, and I have lost money. I have had my pick over money or drugs in my earnings, and guess what I chose?

During the peak of my cocaine addiction, I began seeing an old boyfriend who knew me a few years prior. He always thought of me as a good girl compared to the other girls he knew, even when I was smoking weed every day. When I was fifteen, he would tease me in front of his friends because I wouldn't even say curse words or look at dirty movies. I had no interest, and the attention was embarrassing. But I liked that he viewed me as a good girl.

That one was the opposite of my first serious boyfriend, Hunter. He knew better than to attempt to control me. He would go to bed hours before me while I stayed up with his friends, playing cards. I believe he never would've thought four years prior that I would one day become who I was in the summer of my eighteenth year. I also believe that he gave me grace when I failed him as a girlfriend and as a friend during that time because he knew me before my addiction. He knew the heart that existed beyond the cold exterior.

JESUS LOVES THE BAD GIRLS, TOO

One of the Pharisees invited Jesus to have dinner with him, so he went to the Pharisee's house and reclined at the table. When a woman who had lived a sinful life in that town learned that Jesus was eating at the Pharisee's house, she brought an alabaster jar of perfume, and as she stood behind him at his feet weeping, she began to wet his feet with her tears. Then she wiped them with her hair, kissed them and poured perfume on them. When the Pharisee who had invited him saw this, he said to himself, "If this man were a prophet, he would know who is touching him and what kind of woman she is—that she is a sinner." Jesus answered him, "Simon, I have something to tell you." "Tell me, teacher," he said. "Two men owed money to a certain moneylender. One owed him five hundred denarii, and the other fifty. Neither of them had the money to pay him back, so he canceled the debts of both. Now which of them will love him more?" Simon replied, "I suppose the one who had the bigger debt canceled." "You have judged correctly," Jesus said. Then he turned toward the woman and said to Simon, "Do you see this woman? I came into your house. You did not give me any water for my feet, but she wet my feet with her tears and wiped them with her hair. You did not give me a kiss, but this woman, from the time I entered, has not stopped kissing my feet. You did not put oil on my head, but she has poured perfume on my feet. Therefore, I tell you, her many sins have been forgiven—for she loved much. But he who has been forgiven little loves little." Then Jesus said to her, "Your sins are forgiven".

Luke 7:36-48

HELP

It wasn't until November of 2004 that I called on God at nineteen years old. What led me to finally ask for help? Three months passed me by with me sleeping all day, every day. I lived in my bed. I had been so depressed; I didn't open up a single piece of mail for over three months. The only thing that got me out was hearing that a friend with coke was going to be in town. That was the pit of the pits. Inside I felt the closest thing to what hell could feel like.

Separation from God. All black. Complete darkness. A living nightmare.

Thinking back on all the crazy things I had been doing, putting inside my body, messing up my brain's equilibrium and slowly killing myself with leaves me grateful to just be alive.

WAKING UP

I had a cruise planned with a friend in December of 2004, a month after asking God for help. I stayed in bed the first two days of the cruise because I stayed up all night doing coke before we left. I have only been on one cruise in my life and it was amazing when I finally got out of bed, even in my depressed state. That cruise was only about a month after I asked for help.

When I came back from the cruise, I opened all my mail and handled what ended up being at least twenty bad checks. That was a pain to fix because I had to go to each place where they were written and make it right. I couldn't just pay the overcharges and be done with it.

The bank had been trying to notify me that my account was over drafting. But since I didn't open my mail, how would I know? I finally gave up on college months prior. What a wasted life I was in.

GOD AT WORK

Two months after asking God for help, I regained strength enough to get a job. Behind the scenes of my life at this time, my mother and aunt Amy had been praying for people to reach out to me in the bar where I got a job bartending. They knew I was turned off by religion. They knew I wanted nothing to do with what I had seen of God, but they also knew I had asked God for help on my own a few months prior and was praying, which was a good start.

I don't remember the first man's name that touched my heart in March of 2005, but I remember what he said. He said he could read eyes. I asked, "Oh yeah? So what do mine say?"

He replied, "Your eyes tell me that you're just a good girl who's trying to be bad."

I brushed it off as if I wasn't touched, but I called my brother as soon as I left work and told him. It meant a lot to me that someone still saw me as a good girl at a time when I thought I could never be viewed that way again.

The next one told me about this book they were reading in his men's Bible study group, as he drank a Budweiser out of a glass. He said he wanted me to read it. He came back a few days later with a copy of *The Purpose-Driven Life*.

THAT NIGHT

The night I decided I was done with coke and I finally stuck to it was June of 2005, when I was twenty years old. It started off with me taking a few blue Xanax, and it turned into a total of nine by the time my drug binge ended. Shortly after the pills set in, I got the bright idea to get some coke. When the coke ran out, there was no other option available to me but crack.

A few days later, I was laying in bed so depressed over what I had done that night I smoked crack. Deep down I have always been a good girl, no matter who I was pretending to be or who I was trying to hurt by being bad, and I couldn't let that night go.

I opened my bible, praying God would give me a verse, and I opened my bible directly to this scripture. It said, "Know this, God has even forgotten some of your sin" (Job 11:6, NIV). That was exactly what I needed to hear at that moment, and no other version says it the same.

In the end, I realized speed was never my friend. Every time I would come down, because of the state of misery I would be in, I would say to my friends who didn't do it, "This is the last time ever, I swear."

They would say, "Yeah right, Celia, you say that every time."

I would go through close to a whole roll of tissue paper, blowing my nose, when I started letting myself come down. I would spend the entire day "recuperating" in bed while my mind was awake but my body needed sleep. My body ached and needed rest, but my mind wouldn't allow it. I put myself and my body through misery just to stay high.

For a few years after quitting, I could just think about crying and have to blow my nose. My nose was not right for a while. Healing takes time. Thank you Jesus, that hell is over. Seriously.

The oldest of my younger sisters knows all of my past. She may not be walking with the Lord as close as I would like to see her doing, but she won't ever be a druggie. And she won't ever feel used if I can help it.

SAW A DOCTOR

Within a few weeks of "that night" in June of 2005, my aunt came over in the afternoon while I was in bed. She said, "Get up. We are going to the doctor." Finally someone said something about seeking medical help because it wouldn't have been me.

We went to a family practitioner, and she prescribed me 10 mg of Lexapro daily. Lexapro is a mild anti-depressant for those who suffer from anxiety and/or depression. I started feeling a lot better when I was sober, and fortunately I was able to quit taking it in the spring of 2007. However, when I quit doing speed, I was left with an overwhelming anxiety, even with the help of the Lexapro. So when I did acid two months later, because of my heightened level of anxiety, it was my worst trip ever.

PANIC/FEAR ATTACKS

If someone has any sort of chemical imbalance or mental illness running in their family, psychedelics can most definitely be deadly. I never thought about committing suicide while on them, but I can see how it happens to others. I never once had a trip where I didn't cry or think I was going to die. It took me five bad trips out of the five times I tripped between mushrooms and acid to finally realize tripping just wasn't my thing.

The last night I tripped, it was the second time I did acid. This was in August of 2005. It was wild. It felt like a roller coaster that I didn't like, although there were some moments that I enjoyed; I can't deny that. For instance, I remember I really liked watching this guy dance. There was this song that he danced to on the diving board that I loved but I haven't heard since. Or maybe I have, and it just doesn't sound the same.

A few moments, seconds, or hours before the dancer guy arrived, I had changed into my friend's T-shirt and shorts to feel more comfortable. I was basically in pajama attire. The trip initially started out just me and my friend. I felt safe with that. But then a bunch of strangers including the dancer guy, who were all pro-trippers or something, came over. It totally changed the dynamic.

This girl came with them who I thought was pretty, and I felt guilty about thinking she was pretty. I felt like the girl was hitting on me, but I think she just wanted to hang out with me. Either way, I remember being terrified of her. I saw something black and evil in nature swirling around on her face. Maybe I do have the gift of discerning between good and bad spirited people.

Or maybe I was just tripping.

The roller coaster of emotions only intensified when I hit the "peak" of my trip. I realized I couldn't handle it any longer. I got really hot, and I went into the pool to feel some sort of relief. When I stepped out, it felt like a wave of anxiety and pressure came flooding over me, and then I passed out on the concrete. I thought I died. It was a panic attack on acid. Three out of the five times I tripped, my body reacted to psychedelics in that way. The last time was the worst.

I wasn't completely unconscious for very long, but when I came to I couldn't function. I could barely hear and feel everyone around me talking about calling the hospital. I couldn't talk or open my eyes. I thought I was in a coma or paralyzed. Everything was all black. It was very surreal.

WHAT DID GOD HAVE TO SAY?

What brought on the fear/panic attack was the dancing guy telling me to go sit by the pool by myself and see what God had to tell me. He told me to do that because I had just expressed my concern that I couldn't make up my own thoughts. I had told him that I was worried because I wasn't thinking anything. I could only think what I heard them say. I couldn't say anything out loud like they were and join the conversation. I didn't like that and found it scary that I was depending on them to have my own thoughts.

When I went and sat by myself, what God had to say was also scary. I now know not to ever doubt God is always with me, in every situation. At that time it was pressed upon my heart that I was not where I should be in life at all. That night I was overcome with this sense that things were so wrong that I think it was too much for my brain to handle on acid.

Every time I did psychedelics, I told my friends during my trip that I was never doing drugs again. I would say I was going to be a good girl from then on and focus on school if it would only end.

It was always funny to everyone how I would always say that with all seriousness, but then as they would pass me a bowl of pot to smoke, they would laughingly ask, "Have you quit smoking weed yet?"

I always assured them that I was quitting after it was all over, but I never did. I believe I always had a conscience, and being on something like acid, it only intensified.

There were two different occasions, one before and one after my last trip, where I was high on pot and I fainted from the panic attack in the same way I reacted to LSD and mushrooms. Marijuana raises your blood pressure, and if your body has already went to a certain level of shock or panic, which mine did on psychedelics, it is easier to go there again even without the initial drug or situation that caused it. Both times, it was a result of me overthinking something that made me feel nervous. People have always told me I think too much. Even stoned, I couldn't chill like everyone else.

Moral of the story: I've realized that drugs are not my friends. They are not good for my serotonin levels. They don't make me happy in the long run. And for me, it took being off of them for a while to see how they were holding me back.

FINAL WAKE-UP CALL

I know I didn't start Chapter 2, which was "Day 2" of The *Purpose-Driven Life* until September of 2005. I didn't pick it up until one of my last wake-up calls. That wake-up call involved me going in the kitchen to eat breakfast and looking out the window in shock at my wrecked car.

The night before, I went to a club, had around ten shots of liquor, danced until the club closed, and then left to go home. On the way back home, I wrecked my car by running into the guard rail which spun me into the grassy median. I immediately got back on the interstate as if nothing had happened, went through Krystal's drive thru to order food, saw a cop car who was scoping out my fresh wreckage and who thankfully got called away before my food came out. When I made it home I went straight to bed and passed out.

I didn't wake up with any memory that a wreck had happened the night before till my momaw and I both noticed it while I was eating cereal from the kitchen window. At that time, I broke down crying. That got my attention as far as seriously abusing alcohol.

Yes, coke and I were done that summer. I started taking an anti-depressant, and things began to look up. The acid trip where I freaked out and had to be held all night like an infant by my friend to not faint again was finally over. Thank God. No more coke, no more mushrooms or acid. I wasn't in a deep, dark state of depression like I was the previous November when I asked God for help, but I was still getting stoned and self-medicating. I still needed more help.

This is what spoke to my heart in *The Purpose-Driven Life* at that time:

The title of "Day 2" was "You are not an accident."

> "You were made by and for God-- and until you understand that, life will never make sense. Every other path leads to a dead end."
>
> Rick Warren, The Purpose Driven Life

CHURCH

My aunt and cousins had been going to New Beginnings of Jasper, Tennessee. They had been trying to get me to go, but I was against it. Even though I was praying and seeking the Lord, I wasn't into what I had seen of churches in the past. The people who I had grown up around in my Baptist church were the ones who turned on me and my mother. I didn't respect hypocrites, and I didn't want to go to church and be a part of the hypocrisy I grew up witnessing when I was still smoking weed every day.

But I ultimately gave in and started going after my wreck that I didn't remember. I had heard I was on their prayer list, but I didn't know it was one that was put in front of the church with a projector. I was at the top of their list when I first started going. Where I am today I would find that embarrassing, but where I was back then it made me feel loved.

After a few months, I grew closer to the Lord and got completely clean—no drugs, no inappropriate relationships, and no alcohol even. My name eventually fell off their prayer list on the front projector, too, by that time.

I believe by getting closer to the Lord, what was dark in my life had to flee. I wanted God and I made that clear to Him in prayer. And because I truly reached out and humbled myself that evening when I asked for help in a state of desperation, there was nothing standing in the way. There wasn't any pride or any of my self left for I was dwindling away. I knew if I didn't ask for help, I would die. I submitted to Him because I was all out of options.

But regardless of why I went back to Him, and how unfaithful I was with my back turned on Him, He welcomed me back with open arms and began His work of redeeming His daughter. When you truly want Him, for whatever reason you do, He doesn't hold out on His children.

JUST FACE IT

The only way I lived back then was focusing on the moment at hand and making sure my needs were met rather than being concerned with my future. My madness on drugs lasted two years, but it felt like a lifetime. Only two years of my life was a complete and utter wreckage, and Satan tells me it defines me. It wasn't until now that I realized it doesn't.

If you haven't realized it yet, the truth is you can't escape reality, so don't even bother running from it. If you're reading this now, you either (a) already know this firsthand like me, (b) have never felt like you needed to do that, or (c) you are running now.

If you are running from reality now, you are in a position to make a wise decision. You need to seek help. I never received counseling growing up, when I know that would have helped me. Talking to someone is the best, seriously. It's crazy how hard it is to simply ask for "help" from God or anyone for that matter. Face it, if it wasn't so hard, you would have already asked.

If you are where I once was, your life depends on it. Please be smarter than me. Don't wait as long as I did to humble yourself and ask for help. I lost years with my family that I will never be able to get back.

If you are running now, you only have two options. You will eventually have to face reality, or you will die. And the longer you wait, the worse that reality is going to be when you are finally forced to face it.

Choose freedom. Choose laughter. Choose sunny skies. Choose innocence. Choose a future. Choose life.

If you are finding yourself in a "pit" as you read this, and you haven't given your life to Christ yet, this is your new day. Your new life begins now. All you have to do is ask Him into your heart and pray for God to get you out. And He will, just as He did for me. But it won't be easy breezy, and it may take years like it did me. Breaking free from any kind of bondage is not easy, and it will be a fight.

A fight for your life. A fight for your soul. A fight for your freedom. A fight that pulls everything inside of you out into the open. A fight worth dying to your "self" for.

I know complete restoration of your life is possible for you if you need it. I know this because it happened for me.

> *"I've wiped the slate of all your wrongdoings. There's nothing left of your sins. Come back to me, come back. I've redeemed you."*
>
> Isaiah 44:22, The Message

FORGIVENESS, COMPASSION, AND DIVINE INTERVENTION

It really doesn't matter if the person who hurt you deserves to be forgiven. Forgiveness is a gift you give yourself. You have things to do and you want to move on.

Anonymous

I know I could never be a professional counselor. How could I separate myself from hearing someone else's pain and it not hurt me, too? But if either of my two counselors in the past were to have cried with me during one of my stories, I would have been a bit concerned.

Licensed professionals have to maintain an emotional boundary with their clients if they want to be good at what they do. And from what I hear, it is something that their education doesn't teach them. They have their place in this world, and now I have mine too. For I believe I have truly found my calling—I can love and write others without bounds.

"The heart that goes out of itself gets larger and fuller."

Horace Mann

FORGIVENESS

I was recently questioned if I had I forgiven the last person who was abusive toward me when I was twenty-one years old. Forgiveness, for the most part, comes easy for me if the person is remorseful. I knew in his heart of hearts, he didn't want to do the things he did to me. Needless to say, I forgave that boy years ago.

During the short time we were together, I put up with verbal and physical abuse. So naturally, I understand the women who do that. I don't judge them as I have heard others do, because I know the underlining reason why they do it. But there are no shades of gray when it comes to violence.

When it first started happening, I was told it was going to get worse and that I needed to leave, but I didn't listen. There were only some small bruises behind my bottom lip and on my face from being slapped. Add a few big bruises on my arm from being punched after me calling him a name during a fight, and that still wasn't bad enough to make me leave. Neither was being manhandled, slapped, and pushed around every time he drank, which was every day. I thought I could control him and his drinking, but I thought wrong.

He never showed his violent side until we married. I was in that relationship for the rest of my life, as far as I was concerned. I was determined to not give up on him. Leaving him in his illness to suffer alone was never part of the plan.

He would wake up in the morning after his alcohol binges with the shakes. I knew it was an actual addiction for him because I have never experienced an alcohol withdrawal, and I have been drunk a great deal in my years. My personal experience with addiction is that it is something you can't overcome without a fight. And he wasn't willing to do that. Nothing was worth the fight, not me, himself, or our marriage that was soon annulled.

THE DOOR INCIDENT

God speaks to my heart. Anytime I act on the impressions, everything flows. It was May of 2006 that the door incident occurred. I was twenty-one years old.

The fight started over our cell phones. He had a friend over who cowardly ran off and didn't even call for help when he started getting violent. He first threw me down to the ground in the kitchen causing me to get whiplash from the back of my neck hitting the bottom of the cabinets. Then, he drug me into the bedroom where he began hitting me. I actually had pepper spray that I kept as protection because of his violent outbursts. At this point, I admit I used it on him to get him off of me. But, it didn't even slow him down. It only infuriated him further.

Then, he threw the bedroom door at me from across the room in a raging fit. The first time he threw the door at me, I shielded my face and head the best I could, but it still made impact. The second time, he came closer to me and lifted the door up and bashed me in the back of my head with it again. In that position, I could only duck, which didn't shield anything.

When I stood up after the impact, I immediately panicked. Blood was coming down my clothes from the back of my head and my face. Scalp wounds cause the most bleeding, so there was a good bit of that. The side of my face immediately bulged out nearly the size of a baseball. The blood was something I wasn't used to, neither was a knot the size of a baseball on my face.

When I stood up and saw the blood, I started crying and said to him, "Look at what you did." That probably wasn't the best thing to do. But really, what was best in that situation? Get out then and there, right? That wasn't an option because he wasn't letting me leave, and he wasn't being remorseful. I was accustomed to bruises from abuse, but never blood. When the blood didn't seem to faze him, it scared me even more.

He then grabbed and drug me into the bathroom where he forced me into the shower to clean up because the mess was "disgusting." Before getting in the shower, I was in a state of panic, assuring him, "It is okay, baby, really. I'm not mad." I was trying to trick him into calming down, and I did not succeed.

His response was, "Oh no, no. You've messed with the wrong one!"

While in the shower, where I just stood in shock—I was terrified. I didn't even clean the mess because I could only stand there frozen. I had no game plan in mind, no way out. I didn't know what to do. It wasn't that I couldn't take what had just happened because I was still standing—the impact didn't kill me.

Although I was processing the events and was shook up from them, that part was over. It was the overwhelming fear of what was going to come next that had me terrified.

A few minutes after he put me in the shower, he came back in and pepper sprayed me while yelling and slapping me. When he walked out, my heart sunk. It was at that moment I realized he wasn't going to let me leave. There was no hope or chance. This was it. I truly felt I wasn't going to live through the experience because I didn't see any way out. And to this day, I still don't believe there was going to be if Satan had his way.

As I stared down at the drain, crying out to God in my heart and out loud, I knew that was how it was all going to end for me. I still hadn't reunited with my dad. I was far from restoration and feeling redeemed. I wasn't a college graduate. I was off drugs and in church trying to live right, but there I found myself in another pit of despair.

What I did have that I wasn't as sure of as I am today is the unexplainable, undeniable, almighty God on my side.

At a very specific moment in time while staring at the drain, He told my heart in response to my cries for help in the shower to "go now." It wasn't a panicked urging; it was calm, and it was sure of itself. And it came out of nowhere from a God who knew He was in control of that moment and those to come. That would be our precious God for you. I know it was Him and only because I listened, am I alive writing you today.

As soon as my heart heard, "Go now" in response to my cries out to Him, I left the shower on and tiptoed out of the bathroom with only a towel on. As I shut the door behind me, I saw he was less than ten yards away from me on the balcony, fooling with his cell phone. I found a place to hide in the dining room corner as I waited for him to check on me in the shower so I could escape. I could see the door to exit, and it was unlocked. I was relieved because that would save me the time to unlock it, which I needed. When he started walking toward the bathroom to check on me, I knew it was my time. As soon as he turned the knob and took his first step into the bathroom, I ran to my freedom.

As I watched the police take him away, I actually felt guilty. They said he was passed out asleep when they went in to get him. He told me he didn't remember doing any of what he did and that he had blacked out. To this day, I will never know the truth, so I can only trust what my heart believes to be true—that he didn't.

If one could see how remorseful he was after the incident, maybe I would appear a little less out of my mind for going back to him only four days later. But still, I definitely see the craziness myself. He would cry and be so ashamed. He would promise to go to alcohol and anger management classes. But when the time would come, he would skip. I even went to a few with him for support.

I've already mentioned that he never once got violent with me when he was sober, and I'll say it again. It was the alcohol that activated the rage within him. One night, I had to pick him up from a house where people had ganged up on him and beat him terribly. He told me once that he thought he took it out on me because I was the only person he could do that with since he was passive with everyone else.

THE DAY AFTER

The day after the "door incident," I went to Pastor Dan Walker's house of New Beginnings Church to talk. I had four staples in the back of my head, whiplash from being thrown across the kitchen floor, the sclera of my eye was red, and there was a hematoma protruding from the side of my face reaching to my eye. The hematoma went down in size over time, but it lasted over a year. There is still a small dent on the right side of my face to this day. And there are far worse cases of abuse than that, such as death.

I relived the experience and sought counsel. We had been going to see Pastor Dan for marital counseling. He knew our situation, and had heard and seen enough. He said God wouldn't want me standing in front of a loaded gun, and that is what I would be doing by staying. His counsel was to divorce him. Biblically speaking, adultery is the only grounds for divorce. He committed adultery by choosing his rage and addiction over me.

I have totaled four cars and even went to juvenile for four days when my first boyfriend and I got pulled over with seven ounces of pot in my car. They didn't initially take me to jail but when I went to bail him out with a check from my mother and stoned with pot in my purse they did. And none of that was scary in comparison. The night I escaped, I have never been more scared in all my life.

The hardest thing to learn in life is which bridge to cross and which to burn.

David Russell

SPIRITUAL WARFARE

The enemy possessed someone to repeatedly wrong the man I married when he was only a child. And that enemy was in full control of him when he was drunk. The enemy in me and the enemy in him fed off of each other. If there is such a thing as soul mates, he was Satan's version of mine. Satan couldn't have sent me a better match.

No one deserves to be physically or verbally abused. What makes people do it, and what makes people put up with it? Why is there so much evil in the world? I thought God was in charge.

God is very much in charge, from the beginning and until the end. However, there is an enemy who is out to kill, steal, and destroy us (John 10:10).

He has already lost and knows he is going down on judgment day. He is trying to take as many souls with him because he knows how it hurts God's heart.

We can't see our Creator, and we can't visually see the spiritual realm, but it is there. It is nothing to be scared of if you are a sold-out believer to Christ because we can take authority over the enemy in Jesus's name. And if you aren't a believer, it is still nothing to be scared of because you will be completely oblivious to Him at work in your life.

The closer you walk with the Lord, the more you can expect to notice and be annoyed by His attacks. Since I think on the bright side, my thoughts are, *Well, at least I know I am serving Him in a mighty way.* There has to be some kind of jealousy going on; I must be doing something right.

You can deny the existence of demons, but they are real. How else could he turn into a different person before my eyes? I know I don't need any convincing because of my own personal experience. I had this inner drive to hurt myself for years. That was not of God; that was a drive from Satan. I never had that drive until I told God to go away as a child, and I no longer have that drive now. Coincidence? Not quite.

Whereas God placed desires inside my heart that bring me life and beauty, Satan placed desires inside of me that were making me rot away before my time. He made me ugly on the inside and ugly on the outside, too. The drugs caused the impurities I was ingesting to seep out of my pores, and over time it resulted in severe acne. Combine my acne with obsessive picking, which was one of the other side effects of the drugs I was using, and I was left with a horrible complexion.

"For our struggle is not against flesh and blood, but against the rulers, against the powers, against the world forces of this darkness, against the spiritual forces of wickedness in the heavenly places" (Ephesians 6:12, NASB).

WRONG ONE AND WRONG TIME

My last wake-up call, when I wrecked my car, was in August of 2005. I got completely clean and started going to church. I had just begun recovering when I met him; I was doing so well. I met him in February of 2006 and I married him only three weeks later.

I married the wrong one, but I didn't sleep with him before marriage. I know what you're thinking. You're probably thinking that anyone can wait three weeks. I agree, but I know that my heart was in the right place. But obviously, my mind still needed a lot of healing.

Who in their right ever-living mind meets a guy and marries him three weeks later, especially when he is on intensive probation from alcohol and drug-related charges? I was not naïve to that fact that he had assaulted cops, kicked the window in a cop car out when they were taking him away before, and just got out of jail when we met. But when he told me he got saved in jail, it was my green light.

When I looked at him, I saw he was just a wounded soul like my own. I felt like I could show him that I was once in his shoes, tell him my pain and what I had been through and encourage him to overcome, too. He was my project.

Although I never struggled with rage, I understood him. He had his childhood stolen from him. I knew what that felt like, and I also knew what it felt like to feel misunderstood. I knew what it felt like to not want to do things that were bad but be driven to do them anyway. I knew what hating myself felt like. We both knew how worthlessness felt.

After all, the same thing that did it to me did it to him.

I've learned that this caretaking behavior of mine was all rooted from my childhood. I was a caretaker to my mother's emotional needs growing up. I was recreating a relationship I was familiar with, a relationship where I met their needs in order for them to meet mine—a codependent relationship where I had the power and did the caretaking because I was the stronger one. And in return, I received love.

BRIGHT SIDE

Will I always be affected by the pain of my past? I can honestly say I am over that whole ordeal, but what about the things from my childhood? Will the tears ever cease from all of that? The truth is, the well eventually runs dry. Although the pain affects who I am and who I become, I am not negatively affected forever if I allow myself to experience the uncomfortable feelings and grieve for however many seasons it takes.

Personally, as far as my past suffering goes, I don't want my future children to know that their mother suffered abuse like that. And I don't want others to know that I still do sometimes in other ways. But now that we're getting real, don't we all suffer in some way or another?

Regardless of what I want, my children will not grow up sheltered from my past. They will know what I have been through, and my daughter will never feel what I have felt. And just maybe she will never feel it, because I will know what she needs emotionally from both of her parents to not ever go there. And the truth is, I will only know in the deepest part of my knowing what she will need, because I know what I would have needed. See, there is always a bright side.

GRAHAM AND SHARON

At the court hearing in November of 2006, when the chancellor granted me an annulment, the moment he said my ex's full name and dissolved what was I ran out in tears. That was the morning before a night left alone, with my thoughts wishing for death. If it weren't for my cousins, Graham and Sharon's divine intervention, I would've still been going to visit that boy in jail and sticking with him through the two years he was sentenced.

Before they intervened, I was allowing him to control me while he was in jail by making sure I was home at certain times when he would call throughout the day. I would go to every visit and write letters while remaining loyal to our marriage. I didn't have a job, and I was stuck with hospital bills from the abuse and our bills to pay all by myself since everything was in my name. My credit score dropped. I was in a major bind.

Graham and Sharon said I could live with them at their house, help me pay my bills, help me get me a job, and Graham would be my lawyer and hopefully get me an annulment under one condition: no further contact with him. I was backed into a corner. I had no other choice.

When I had to stop seeing him and writing him without telling him why, I felt like I abandoned him. I told him I would wait on him before he went to jail, and I meant it with all of my heart. But I didn't intentionally lie. God intervened on my behalf through Graham and Sharon, and even through the incident itself.

He had overlapping sentences before we met. One of the sentences he was serving was an eleven month, twenty-nine day probation that ended the day after the abuse. If the incident happened two days later, he would have never had to go to jail. Therefore, I wouldn't be alive today because I wouldn't have had to leave him.

THE GIFT OF COMPASSION

I have always had an overwhelming compassion for others. There was this boy in elementary school who all the kids would tease and torment. I was his only friend, and I know wherever he is right now, he remembers me.

When I won a watch in sixth grade for placing second in the Drugs Abuse Resistance Education essay contest, I gave it to him, and his gratitude was so precious. The Christmas presents for him started in third grade, with my mother's money, of course. I remember a classmate asking me why I gave him presents, as if something were wrong with me. I didn't care to be different then. I didn't care to be me. My faith in God back then wasn't as intense as it is now, but I know the Jesus I had already asked into my heart was loving that boy through me.

Sometimes our greatest gifts can be misused if we are not discerning on how and when it is appropriate to apply our gifts. God doesn't want His creation to be abused in any way, verbally or physically. And He didn't create us to be doormats, either.

FIGHT FOR YOUR FREEDOM

Don't be blinded by the sun when you look to the heavens, for the stars are well beyond it, for to appreciate such beauty, patience is your virtue.

Anonymous

When going through recovery, depending on the length of time one abandoned themselves, add the level of pain, amount of drugs, alcohol, and bad choices they made, and the result is that they are left with the uncomfortable reality that they are not going to feel "right" for a while.

In my case, I self-medicated for years. I shut down emotionally. The state I found myself in was the state in which I initially abandoned myself since I decided to take matters into my own hands instead of seeking professional help for the overwhelming pain I was feeling.

I medicated in a number of ways. I used relationships to temporarily relieve the ache. And I used drugs. I used anything I could get my hands on in order to not feel the ache.

All that I used as a means to "make the pain go away," I had to eliminate from my life completely for the time being, especially relationships when they were abusive and/or codependent. The Merriam-Webster medical dictionary defines codependency as a psychological condition or a relationship in which a person is controlled or manipulated by another who is affected with a pathological condition (as an addiction to alcohol or heroin).

When I returned to a sober reality from my coma, I discovered that the world had moved on without me in it. I had been living in my own reality, and I then realized which reality I should have been living in.

I discovered that those who I was actually more intelligent than "academically" had gone on to college, graduated, and were on their way to begin their master's degree. While I, on the other hand, still had a ways to go to graduate college.

My skin broke out because of all the speed and it was very difficult for me to get it back under control. The cigarettes I smoked caused some premature wrinkles. I felt worn out and dried up. And I was only nineteen-years-old. But I was alive and on the path to recovery with a bright future beyond the tunnel. So for that alone, little did I know I had every reason to grin and bear it.

> *Have patience with all things, but chiefly have patience with yourself. Do not lose courage in considering your own imperfections, but instantly set about remedying them, every day begin the task anew.*
>
> St. Francis of Sales

GET BACK WITH YOURSELF

When I was twenty-four, I met this lady at the YMCA. I was getting ready to go out, and she was cleaning the locker room. We got into a conversation about our dreams and ambitions. At the time, I was interested in life coaching. I told her that I would probably wait until I was thirty to start coaching because no one would want to take advice from me because of my age. Her response was, "When you talk you, speak like you know what you're talking about. People will listen to what you have to say, regardless of your age."

I was in shock. I wanted to jump up and down out of excitement right then and there. And knowing me, I probably did. *I am the type of person others would listen to? Unbelievable,* I thought. I was obviously still identifying with my former days.

Sure, people listened to me because they had to if I was around. I have always been a little bossy because I am the oldest of all my siblings and I take after my dad. I am most definitely an alpha female.

Although I was the "command attention" type and people listened to me, I don't think any friends of my past knew how intelligent I was capable of being. They never got to see that side of me. I even forgot about that side of myself over time.

Being "Celia, the smart girl," didn't feed my ego. While I was on drugs and living in sin, my ego fed off of the physical compliments. That is why I dressed like a girl who was seeking attention. Being smart didn't spark the opposite sex's attention in the group I was in.

When I was growing up, I received a lot of academic awards. I was known for being the teacher's pet and an academic overachiever. In fourth grade, my teacher made the suggestion to my mom that I skip fifth grade. That was the same teacher my childhood boyfriend said I "cried" over when we found out she was leaving the school. And just for the record, I never cried about her leaving.

I would cry over B's, though, up until I was fifteen. And I still have one of my report cards that showed I had all 100's in my subjects, but in science I had a 97. Why couldn't they all be 100's? And that teacher wasn't going to give me an undeserved grade just to make me happy. I didn't ask her to do that, but I remember wishing she had. At the time, she ruined my day.

I am that same girl, just older, and with an interesting life story, to put it lightly.

> *The great thing in this world is not so much where we are, but in what direction we are moving.*
>
> Oliver Wendell Holmes

DOUBLE-MINDEDNESS

> *Jesus said, "So then because you are lukewarm, and neither cold nor hot, I will spew you out of my mouth."*
>
> Revelation 3:16

From the age of twenty-one to January of 2011, at twenty-five, I was a "fence straddler." I wasn't sold out completely to God, but I was just good enough to where I could look down on the bad kids and pretend I had never been there. My double-mindedness left me mentally drained. I knew I was wrong. When I was wild, I was wild, and I didn't pretend to be good. When I finally got my act together, I wanted to party here and there and still benefit from having a relationship with Christ.

It was exhausting loving God just enough to where He was protecting me, but not enough to not feel like the fake hypocrites I had seen my whole life. The hypocrites are the ones who hurt me as child, and I became one of them. I knew I needed to pick one side or the other. I didn't respect myself for being a hypocrite as much as I didn't respect myself when I was wild.

James sums it up in James 1:6-8 (NIV), "But when you ask, you must believe and not doubt, because the one who doubts is like a wave of the sea, blown and tossed by the wind. That person should not expect to receive anything from the Lord. Such a person is double-minded in all they do."

FRIENDS

When I really wanted to change, there was a point in my life where I had to cut some of my friends completely out of my life. It sounds harsh, I know. It was the hardest thing for me to do because I didn't want to hurt anyone. But I had reached a point where I realized I was never going to get ahead and break free of things I didn't want to do if I kept surrounding myself with people who encouraged the very things I was trying to change within myself.

When my last boyfriend and I broke up at twenty-three, I started drinking heavily again. I consider going out four nights a week and getting trashed a drinking problem.

When I realized I needed to change, I cut all my party friends off. My thing is this, if the only thing we have in common is drugs and alcohol, then we are not truly friends. Because when taking any of the above out of the equation, what were we left with? The friendship I developed with my party friends was built upon sand.

Every friend I have told, "I love you" to, I meant it. There are many people I love and still think about, but I am not going to spend my time around them if they aren't edifying. Counselors get paid and so do life coaches. Friends from my past, I would counsel for free. But if they want to just "hang out," I don't typically go there unless it's a special occasion. My parents always told me that someday I would outgrow some of my friends. It is impossible for me not to do that unless I am not growing or we are all growing together.

The relationships I surround myself with now are ones where we mutually encourage and build each other up. I am not called to be emotionally close to anyone that attacks or tears me down. Although I am called to love and minister to them when I can, I am not called to save the world at my own expense.

My mom always blamed the people I hung around for my bad behavior, as most parents do, I am sure. Sometimes she was right, but other times I can get in trouble all by myself.

I thought I was never going to be able to quit smoking pot for good. I would go a year at a time not smoking pot and then break my roll. The last time I did was in June of 2010. I ate so much afterwards that I said, "This is it. I am finally done forever. I have no reason to be doing this unless it is for medicinal purposes and I live in the west, where it is legal."

When I came home after getting stoned, my mom looked at me and knew immediately. She asked where I had been, and I told her that I went and got some all by myself and I smoked it all by myself. No one could be blamed but me. She told me getting stoned didn't compliment my personality, and she was right. That was the first time in my life I ever hung around her high, and I discovered she was just as cool, if not cooler, than all the other people I used to hang out with.

Although I wasn't influenced to smoke pot that final time, when I first got off coke, I had to change my phone number and erase a lot of my contacts. I didn't want to be tempted to use any of those resources in the future in case I relapsed. I changed my phone number on purpose two or three times. It was just easier that way to detach.

At first, I couldn't even go near people that did coke. I knew if I was around them, I would probably be the one to bring it up, and we would get some. Then, I got to where I could go near them, but never when they were planning on doing it or having it around. I knew I had beaten the addiction when I was drunk on Halloween in 2008, and not only was I around it, but I watched people do it. I saw it for the first time in years as the people I was with did lines on a chest of drawers in a bedroom. Even drunk, I wasn't tempted to do any. I was finally over it. I was so proud of myself.

When I was ready to give up getting drunk, I couldn't even go to a classy bar. Why? Because I had the weakness to get wasted, and if I was around others who were getting trashed, I would have gladly joined in on the fun.

For a while, I would isolate myself and sit at home on the weekends. That was the only way I could control myself. But as I would sit at home on the weekend, I would be thinking, *There has to be a better way than this.* And there was.

In a matter of weeks I went from zero sold-out Christian friends to two. And within that month, I added a few more to the list. When you associate yourself with like-minded people, it isn't impossible to go out into the world and not sin. Although we're not "of it" (John 17:16, NIV), we're still living in the world while we're here. Personally, it was impossible for me to do that alone at first.

Some may say I have no business being in a bar at all. Well, take that up with Jesus. He was friends with the sinners because He could handle it. He could be around them and not sin.

Now, I may be seen somewhere I deem classy drinking a glass or two of wine with a glass of water in between, and I may even have a cocktail or a beer. But I won't ever be seen intoxicated again, because I make the effort to manage my weaknesses.

CLARITY

In order to improve myself, I needed to be clear about where I was. Then I decided what I would want to be like if I could be like anyone else in the world. It took years to achieve it, but now I know I can be any type of person I wish to be if I work hard enough. I wanted to be all smiles. I wanted to go from feeling like trash to a treasure, and I did. I was never going to be who I wanted to be until I took the steps necessary to get there. I needed to be clear about who I wanted to be and where I wanted to go.

I wanted to be taken seriously, so I changed and over time, people viewed me differently. But I had to start viewing myself differently first. For how I perceived myself affected others' perceptions of me.

All the clutter in my life such as debt, unhealthy relationships, and partying robbed me of my clarity. I would've always been reading books to help me get better instead of writing my own if I didn't rid myself of the nonsense.

> *For the road goes on and is smoother, And the pause in the song is a rest,*
> *And the part that's unsung and unfinished Is the sweetest and richest and best.*
>
> From "The Bend in the Road" by Helen Steiner Rice

HONOR YOUR PARENTS

Honey, you have never ceased to amaze me.

My dad

My dad was living his life in Pennsylvania with my stepmom and three brothers while staying connected as much as he could. I started flying by myself to visit him two to three times a year when I was five.

My mom always bought me new clothes before my visits. Well this particular time, she forgot to keep an eye on the green-and-white play school scissors she bought to cut my tags off with. We literally went shopping for clothes and headed directly to the airport.

They moved me so many times on that plane ride. I got such a kick out of being a little terror. I wasn't a psycho little girl cutting people; I was just pretending like I would while laughing. I wasn't even being obnoxious about it at first, but as soon as I saw that it was getting me a reaction, I had fun with it.

They eventually moved me by myself near the pilot. He was really nice, and didn't scold me. After all, I was only six at the most. Pretty sure my stepmom thought it was funny, too, when the stewardess told on me. But in my mind at six years old, my only punishment was never getting my scissors returned to me.

MY DAD

My dad is a doctor, and that has always made me feel special. Even at twenty-five, I feel special being the only daughter of a well-respected doctor and businessman. I have the best financial advisor and mentor a twenty-five-year-old female could ask for. He is the most emotionally available man I have ever known when he has the time and energy. He is brilliant. That is who my earthly father is and was always meant to be.

When I ran away at fifteen and lived with him for six months, what I needed but I couldn't express at the time was for my dad to fight as hard as he could and break through the walls I shut him out of. Honestly, he wouldn't have been able to. And that man tried harder than anyone ever has.

I literally shut down on him and couldn't speak. I remember him shaking me and crying, begging for me to just say something. My heart was feeling sorry for him when he wanted me to speak, but I went mute. My mouth was sewn shut. It was dysfunctional and wrong. But it was something that my heart had no control over. I couldn't stop the drive to hurt myself, let alone hurt others.

My dad was confused on how to handle me after my return to Tennessee for a visit turned into me staying. He was fed up with my behavior, and lucky for him, he lived eight hundred miles away. He was showing me tough love by keeping me away and protecting his children by not exposing them to me.

The day he said that he didn't want me to visit because he didn't want his children exposed to me probably wasn't good for me to hear considering it only said to me "you are defective." And he should've come to visit me in Tennessee during those six years we didn't see each other. But out of sight, out of mind.

PAIN VALIDATED

One night when we were talking in October of 2009 when I was twenty-four, right before I started seeing Mr. Harris, he asked me what I was dealing with, and I told him I would lie in bed at night crying myself to sleep over the shame of my past. He asked me, "What is the worst thing you have ever done?" and then started guessing because I wasn't going to tell him. It didn't take him too many guesses until he figured it out. At that point he started yelling, "Do you know whose fault that was, do you know whose fault that was!"

Uncontrollably sobbing, I managed to reply, "No." I was thinking he was about to say my mother, but he said, "It was my fault, Celia, I should've been there. If I had been there, it never would've happened!" And he was right.

All of these emotions came rushing out of me in violent sobs as he spoke those words of life. The rush of emotions was the manifestation of all the shame I harbored inside. Deep shame that I felt was part of my defected existence was finally validated, brought to light, dealt with, shown compassion on, and was then wide open and ready for the Holy Spirit healing that would later ensue.

Hearing his heart of true remorse for what his intentional separation did to me helped heal my heart at twenty-four. My dad continues to breathe life into his only daughter by his affirming words with every phone call.

MOMMY JUDY

I recently wrote a letter to my stepmom, who I have called mom since I was three:

When I came home Saturday night, mom had found things from my childhood (cards, report cards, stories I'd written for school, etc). All of that stuff is either still at ex-dad's or he has thrown it away because when we left we didn't bring anything with us except clothes. Anyways, there were all these cards you sent me growing up. Thank you for being one of my mother figures.

I have quite a few...two of which are these black ladies from work, then there is Sharon, my momaw, and even aunt Anna and aunt Amy at times. I must be one needy 25 year old...but one day I will not only appear grown but I will feel it. Either way, I will always appreciate the women who have emotionally nurtured me throughout my life. My mom just doesn't have it in her but I know if she could, she would.

You have been the most consistent and most available of all the ones I've ever needed. You never needed, depended or relied on me for strength growing up which probably makes me cling to you more because if anything, I've always gotten more from our relationship than I could give. Which if you think about it, that's the way the mother/daughter dynamic should be when a child is growing.

As I grow older and I mature, our dynamic should be more leveled out. But when you talk to me on the phone it hits a spot that needs to be touched...and the same with dad. When things are right with my relationship with you and with dad (and of course God) and I have come to a place of acceptance as far as my mother and our relationship goes, I couldn't feel more whole.

God gave us the people in our lives for a reason. Just because Grandma didn't birth you, doesn't mean God's will wasn't for her to be your mother all along. Because he knew you would need her and she could meet your needs as a mother from childhood to adulthood.

With all this said, I'm going to get back to work. I just wanted to convey my appreciation for you still being there and for being a positive influence throughout my life and if I had my way... throughout the rest of my years to come. Love you. Have a great rest of your week.

Her response was:

Thank God for waterproof mascara!!! You are too much! Thanks for that message, it means so much to me. I just wish I was a little more mature when you were younger so I could of handled different situations better. I believe everything happens for a reason and just wanted to let you know that having you in my life has made me a better person. I thank God every day for having such a beautiful & wonderful daughter. I love you so much & want nothing but the best for you! Your future is soooo bright I might need to go buy myself a new pair of shades so I can be there to watch it unfold. Have a great day! -Your Proud "Mom."

I love that woman, her beautiful heart and all. While my dad was getting on to me out of frustration after discovering cuts on my arm at fifteen, she just held me and sobbed with compassion. You can't fake that. I can't deny the way her display of compassion touched my heart, even in the cold state it was in.

The day I relived my experiences with my brothers, dad, and stepmom on Christmas in 2006 when I was twenty-one, she got up from the table and wrapped her arms around me and cried with me. When I was little, I would write her about all the things that were going on, and I know she felt helpless. Our relationship wasn't one of perfection. But it is one of restoration and one that I can look back on and say that I know that woman loves me.

MY MOTHER

Everything wonderful about who I am would not be possible without my mother. She may have failed me emotionally growing up, but she has never once made me feel abandoned. And she never hurt me on purpose.

I grew up with her being my older sister, it felt like. I would argue with her like a sister and talk with her like a sister.

I grew up feeling as if I had to validate her, rather than her be my mirror as parents should be to children by telling them their value with positive affirmations and encouragement. But before the messy divorce, I was fine with that because I didn't need her validation. I was strong and I wasn't confused because I knew I was above the madness I witnessed, not part of it.

I didn't need her to be at my softball games and award ceremonies while she was running a successful furniture business. I was independent, and that was our relationship. I was the strong one, and she was the weak one. But we were too close, and she knows that.

When I went through my rebellion, I completely detached from my mom. I went from her being my best friend and who I depended on emotionally, even if I was the one in control of the relationship, to nothing.

I have gotten close to women over the years who would "mother" me. It was an unmet need. I needed a mother more than a friend. She wasn't whole, and she didn't raise a whole daughter. She has always been in a relationship since she got married as a virgin at nineteen. She does not feel whole without a man, and a lot of women don't. I grew up exactly like my mother before I changed. So who am I to judge?

COMPROMISE

Because I detached from our unhealthy mother/daughter relationship, I would develop friendships with women recreating the emotional intimacy that I knew with her. They weren't healthy, they were codependent, and they were not always appropriate.

For a while, I was concerned that I was never going to be happy with a man—that only women could meet my emotional needs. I am just a really sensitive woman, and because of the pain inflicted on me in my past from men, I am scared to show them my heart. I can be my sweet, tender-hearted self with my girlfriends, but with guys I put up this tough, I-don't-care-either-way front. They don't get to see my heart because they represent the ones that broke it, beginning with my dad and ex-dad.

When I was nineteen and I broke up with my first boyfriend, I had a friendship with a girl that I leaned on to replace him. I told Mr. Harris about this and he summed it up perfectly, "Relationships of the same sex can simply be easier because you both know how you operate." He wasn't condoning it at all. He was stating the truth; they can be easier to relate to. I know how to be a friend to a girl, whereas a guy might not know how to give the same support emotionally unless he was raised by women, is naturally gifted in the area of sensitivity, or is truly after a girl's heart.

Compromise is a position I don't want to be in with anyone again. I should never feel like I have to do what people ask me to do to keep them around. I should never sleep with someone for that reason, and I should never put up with abuse because I need that person's company.

I have a voice, and God wants me to speak up for my rights and not be walked upon. He wants me whole. He wants me to be able to stand on my own two feet if something were to happen to my significant other, if there's ever another. Praise God I am finally feeling whole in that area. What a blessing it is to be happy when it's just me and God. When I was little, I was happy without a significant other; don't you remember those days too? Gotta love that kind of beauty.

A LITTLE GRACE

My mother was a young mother. She was a better mother to me than I would have ever been if I were in her shoes. She was recreating the only relationship she knew with her mother and her sister. But guess what? The buck stops here.

I figured out the dysfunction because I hit my rock bottom and had to re-evaluate my entire existence. Thank you, Lord, for my rock bottom; it has made me strong and wise because I was determined to be fixed and learn from every mistake I had ever made and every one that I was going to make in the future. But, the first step was calling on God and my faith in Jesus.

I would have died in my pit without asking God for help. Then He throws me blessing after blessing, rope after rope to get me out and redeem me. I deserve none of what I have. I deserve to have rotted teeth and craters on my face from all the meth I did instead of ice-pick acne scars. I deserve to have had at least one STD in my lifetime. I don't deserve Him.

In *What's So Amazing about Grace?*, Philip Yancey wrote:

Grace does not excuse sin, but it treasures the sinner. True grace is shocking, scandalous.

One of my friends said it best; she said, "I think you have gone through all you have because He knew you could handle it. He didn't allow anyone else to be affected like you in your family because they might not have lived through it to talk about it. He knew you were strong."

My determination and intelligence is why I believe God knew I could handle what I went through. This moment right now is why it was part of His plan. I am His, and my eternal future is secure. And yes, redemption does have stories to tell, doesn't it?

GROW UP

When I was a child, I could blame my issues on my parents all I wanted. Even when I became a teenager, it was still their fault. But when I reached my twenties, the people I met didn't typically care what made me the way I was. Most people viewed me without consideration of what made me that way.

Although I have compassion on the hurting, there are so many people with inspiring stories that I just don't understand the ones who don't strive to be better. There are stories where people came from nothing. They grew up in poverty, and now they are monetarily rich because they worked as hard as they could to make it.

There are women and men who grew up sexually abused and who aren't promiscuous, although I would understand what led them there.

There are those who have gone through more than I have and never once thought to try drugs.

There are those that were sexually abused by someone of the same sex who grew up with an attraction, often secretly, to the same sex, but they choose not to act on it.

And there are even those who were truly born with the predisposition since birth to be attracted to the same sex and you still don't see them living in the sin.

Do you want to know who else I understand? The prostitutes. Whether someone sells their bodies for money, drugs, or love, I can understand how they got there, and I could never judge them for that. And although I will not judge them for wanting to stay there when someone has reached out to them in a loving way and directed them to the truth, I will never understand them.

Wanting to do wrong and being driven to evil are two different things. Even though I was being bad, I wanted to be good. I was in so much bondage that it wasn't easy. I can understand the relapsing, and so can God. He gets us more than we could ever understand ourselves. But I don't understand quitters, and I don't understand why anyone in their heart of hearts would want to be bad if they could help it. I guess I have always been a child of the Light, because darkness never looked good on me nor did it feel good.

DO BETTER

Here is the deal: wherever you find yourself, you don't have to stay there. Yes, you have a reason for being there; you can't help it or you were driven there. But you don't have to stay. If you want to please God, He will give you the grace and ability to overcome any position you find yourself in.

There are those out there who were born with the worst possible hand of cards that anyone has ever been dealt. Your story may be the worst story there has ever been. But there comes a time when you can no longer use your bad hand as an excuse. No matter what hand you are dealt, you can bluff, take your chances, repeatedly fail and one day win at life, all the while with a "losing hand."

TAKE RESPONSIBILITY

Everything that happened to me while I was under the age of eighteen my mother and father are to blame. And they both take responsibility for where they have been at fault.

Although they were to blame for not combining as one force during my rocky childhood, I can no longer play the card of a tough childhood being my reason for being a dysfunctional adult. I do not continue to play that card and expect any earnings, because there aren't any. At twenty-five, you don't receive the same pity and sympathy that a child would. And pity bothers me as an adult, so I don't even consider that an earning.

Bottom line is my parents are human, and they deserve my forgiveness and respect. One of the Ten Commandments is "Honor your father and mother." It is more than a suggestion; it is His command.

ALWAYS SEEK THE BRIGHT SIDE

Do not anticipate trouble, or worry about what may never happen. Keep in the sunlight.

Ben Franklin

The hurting need their cheerleaders, and it just so happens I love to encourage and cheer people on who are struggling. Why is that? Because I know what it's like to have to fight to get well.

I remember what the looks felt like from everyone, even those hiding behind the label of Christianity while exhibiting through their unloving actions that they do not even abide in Him. That's not Jesus. The people who were nicest to me offering compassion during my misunderstood phase were not the majority.

Call it "meant to be" or "everything happens for a reason." Call it predestination. Call it what you wish, but I am glad it happened now that it is all finally over.

"Predestination: the doctrine that everything has been determined in advance by God" (Webster).

Would you ever believe I was once "trash"? Well, at least in my eyes and the world's, I was. And good thing that happened, too, because if not, I wouldn't be able to tell others that feel that way that I know what "trash" feels like and that I know what the looks that "trash" receives on a daily basis feel like, too.

Have you ever felt like people thought you were trash? If not, then skip on to another chapter. If you feel like people think you are trash, it should be pretty comforting to hear from someone who has felt like you before and who doesn't feel like that today. I try to pretend I am talking to myself six years ago. Also, I am far more sensitive than most people. So anything you feel that is negative, it probably felt worse to me.

Would you believe I am still misunderstood? Now my lively and often bubbly nature is judged as lack of maturity. Happy people were annoying to me, too, when I was in misery. But if they only knew that I am just thankful I am not in pain anymore. I am happy that I feel good. My gloomy days are over, and yours will be, too. I have joy, and I have joy about the fact that I have joy. And all that joy is a lot more joyful than most people since I am one of those highly sensitive people.

FEELING GOOD

When life hands us lemons, what do we do? We hopefully make lemonade with them. We turn the bitter into sweet. If you determine to make the best of your situation, you will reach a place where you feel the same as I do about yourself, your past, your life in general, and your future. But it won't happen if you don't make the best of your situation, are in denial about your past, and are still living, breathing, walking, and talking in sin.

I'm sure you don't believe it; I wouldn't have either. But if you follow my "formula," which is giving your life to the Lord and giving yourself time to heal, you will one day find, as well as be thankful for, the reason why everything happens, too.

"But it is for this very reason that I have kept you alive—to show you my power, and so that my name may resound throughout the whole earth" (Exodus 9:16, CJB).

FAILURE

And just in case you may have failed at something or everything, it doesn't make you a failure. Please don't equate who you are by your failures or successes. We need something more rock solid to identify with than that. Even if you are successful, life has no guarantees.

A bonus to failing is that it strengthens you. It gets your mind thinking—or at least let's hope it does. If you're wise, you brainstorm different avenues so you can prevent the failure from happening again. The failure may even cause you to change direction. That would be called a "wake-up call" in *Celia's Eyes*.

Thank God for my failures. And let's thank Him for unanswered prayers while we're at it, too.

I will say this, if it is a "dream" you keep on "failing" at, don't ever give up. Speaking from experience, chasing the dream is such an enjoyable process. You have a calling and a purpose. If it's your very first dream, you may notice that it gives you more focus and clarity than you ever had. As long as you are detaching yourself from the outcome and are open to what that may be, you should find your dream-chasing fulfilling. Personally, I am having the time of my life.

FEAR

Only when you have lost everything, are you then free to do anything. If you have ever lost everything you had, you know that couldn't be truer. At that place, what else did we have to lose?

When you are free, fear doesn't dominate. You aren't held back by the should's or should not's. While trying to get back on my feet, fear was the last of my worries. I had greater things to worry about such as going back to school, getting my driver's license reinstated, setting up payment plans for bills I was stuck paying, paying my hospital bills, seeking restitution for the hospital bills that I shouldn't have had to pay, getting my restitution, finding a job, figuring out how I was going to pay everything with just that job, getting a second job, getting a third job, and going to counseling all at the same time.

On the bright side, when I finally resurfaced from my mess, I felt like a million bucks. Yes, God was on my side, and all glory goes to Him. But I worked my butt off, and I finally caught back up. I know I can conquer anything if I can conquer something that feels impossible, even fear. I let fear motivate me. God doesn't give me a spirit of fear, but of power and of love and of self-control (2 Timothy 1:7, BBE). If I am afraid to do something, I do it just to push myself—as long as it's not dangerous.

I don't allow fear to dominate me like I have in the past. I am not just talking about the fear of being alone and the fear to try something new; I mean the spirit of fear that exists. When I first started writing, I had this overwhelming fear that came over me, causing me to faint. The only time I have had that severe of a panic attack was when I was on acid or mushrooms.

That same fear has been haunting me since I was a child. It was the same fear that spoke so powerfully to my heart at eleven years old, "No matter what you do, you are going to hell. No matter how good you are now, you are going to turn bad and you won't end up in heaven."

That fear made me lie in my bed the rest of the night frozen. I wouldn't let myself touch either side of the racecar bed. The next day, I called my mom crying because of what "it" said. She told me,

"Oh no, don't worry about that." This was before she was "spiritually aware."

I asked my last counselor about that to see if that meant I was crazy. He told me that children with wild imaginations do creative things such as that, and it was normal. That eased my fear of me possibly being crazy.

When the spirit of fear came on me recently, I was scared to the point that I said I wasn't going to write anymore because I instinctively knew why it was happening. Satan didn't want me writing because he wanted to keep me in my chains. He knew that through me writing you, God was delivering me in His own sweet way.

I believe when I was allowed to watch horror movies as I child, I was opened up to Satan attacking me with fear. I'm sure it was those movies I watched with my ex-dad where the fake dolls were the murderers that did me in.

Jesus says we have the authority to cast evil away from us in His name. Needless to say, that stupid fear is no longer an issue, and if it comes on me again, I know what to do. And I won't invite anything like that in my heart, mind, and soul by watching scary movies ever again, even as an adult.

"Good Morning"

Good morning to a new day
A new way of living. A better way of being
For I am real, I am seen
I am heard, And I am free
After all my reaching for the stars, I am now happily resting
in His arms
You see who I am, where I have been and how I have grown
So love me or hate me, you know me

For now, I am known
I move without fear, I live without regret and I hope that you will too
I pray that you will choose the right and the only way, my Love who pursues
By now, you should know if this was meant for you
If so, guess what? He loves you too.

DEAR GOD, I HATE SIN

But, oh dear, we'll never deserve it. No dear, we never could earn it. You've been given innocence again.

Partial Lyrics to "Innocence Again" by Switchfoot

NOISE

Any form of sin creates noise for me. And noise keeps me from hearing Him. Simple as that. When it gets noisy, I pray for God to search my heart and bring to my attention what I am doing outside His will. Then, I repent and move on. That's how it works for me.

When there is less noise in my life and I can hear from Him more clearly, I don't feel so alone. And when I don't feel all alone in life, I have no reason to fear. Without fear present, I am free to live. I am free to be. Those positive feelings make me feel that I am exactly as and where I should be in this moment. I have confidence, and I actually feel really good about myself, unlike back in the day.

PURITY

In Christ, I am told I am pure. But I used to think, "That's great and all, but what about feeling pure?" Although I don't deserve to feel pure, I do. I don't feel dirty; I feel clean. And the season of me grieving over the shame my past brought me has finally passed.

We were created pure, and we were created to remain pure. Even while dwelling in darkness, also known as living in hell, I envied those I saw worshipping God with their pure hearts. Unfortunately, we had so much coming in between us at the time. On that particular Sunday I "waked and baked" prior to church service. Although I was stoned, my heart still wanted to be with Him like the others. And God knew that.

The true, blissful, pleasing, awe-inspiring worship to the one who saved me from an eternal hell and my on earth living hell just doesn't happen without a clean and pure heart.

My hands were held down. My mouth was sewn shut. Tears just couldn't happen. Where was the freedom in that?

Every child is born innocent. It wasn't about what my record looked like. I, in my most natural state, was pure. I was a human made in God's own image. That's why I could only get it back from the one who created me.

And it's not about "being good." He doesn't sit up in heaven with a checklist of what I do right and what I do wrong. So I gave that up. Instead, I focused on Him, and I naturally became less enticed by sin.

HEART RESTORATION

> *"Create in me a pure heart, God, and make my spirit right again."*
>
> Psalm 51:10, NCV

I knew God was purifying my heart when I began grieving over things that I was once desensitized to. Impurity meant nothing to me at one time in my life. But my past actions began to break my heart some time after recommitting my life to Him.

My past started breaking my heart because He gave me a new heart, a heart that was soft and breakable, no longer made of stone. My heart can now be touched, and it offers warmth and love to others. He placed desires inside of me that I would've never wanted when I was living and breathing in sin. I now see things from an entirely different perspective.

If you gave your life to the Lord at an early age, only to turn your back on Him like I did, know this: He will welcome you back with open arms, and you will find the view quite familiar. And if you're anything like me, you just might be relieved.

If home is where the heart is, my home is with Him.

SOUL RESTORATION

I never thought I could get it back. It was more than God just restoring my virginity. You could be a virgin and not feel pure. The world is a nasty place, and sometimes we see things by accident as children that we aren't meant to see, and sometimes even on purpose. I am talking about my soul being in its most precious state—the state God wanted it in for me.

I have tasted, and I have seen. Purity feels best. Why? Because it is what I was always meant to feel. I was meant to feel good, whole, and worthy of love. Because we were made in the image of God, we are capable of literally blowing others away with our radiance. My soul instinctively knew and wanted that, despite what came out of my mouth. But I couldn't lie to myself and ever get free.

I could put up a false, untouchable front for everyone. It's called rejecting others before they could reject and emotionally devastate me. I was cold and hateful. But deep down, I knew it was all a lie, which is partly why I was so miserable. It's calling running from the truth and when you do that, you will never be at peace.

HOLY SPIRIT HEALING

Don't get me wrong, I am still attacked with feelings of shame and inferiority. I know my healing isn't complete because when I am in His presence, often all I can do is cry like a little girl. Not every time now, but for a while it was every day. Healing just takes time.

For me, I see Him visually through my own transformation. I physically feel His presence when I worship or ask Him to draw near. I remember what it felt like when my dad held me like a baby. That is what it feels like when I let my tears out in God's presence.

If I didn't feel it, I wouldn't believe it.

I couldn't feel fully restored until He made my heart feel clean again. The Holy Spirit took it upon Himself to get all the impurities and pain from my past out of me. I didn't ask to be sweetly delivered, but He read my heart.

He has healed my heart, my mind, and my soul. Although I am free, He is not finished with me yet. There was so much internally that needed repair. When the tears pour in His presence, they come from a place of pain. I am not grieving over this or that specifically anymore. I am simply releasing what He apparently wants out of me.

My mom calls it my "spontaneous deliverance" because it isn't an everyday-at-a-certain-time-of-day thing. I believe He is healing my heart from things my mind doesn't even remember, such as my dad leaving when I was only three-years-old. How could I not praise and adore someone who takes away pain which holds me back in life that I wouldn't even know to ask Him to remove?

How I feel about myself on the inside shades my decisions, relationships, and actions toward myself and others. After I cry in His presence, I am that much closer to feeling that none of the things I have been through happened. I haven't felt like I have ever been physically or verbally abused in some time, but I have. I don't feel like I have ever had sex outside of marriage. I don't feel like an outcast. And I don't feel like I have ever done drugs. I feel pure, good, and beautiful on the inside, and I am fully aware I don't deserve any bit of that.

The only thing I am dealing with now is pain from my childhood. He wants it gone. Although I will remember all He has delivered me from, I am not called to keep it inside. He wants the burden of having to carry the heaviness in my heart to cease because He loves me that much. He wants me to feel good. He wants me to have healthy relationships. He wants me to be well. Everything that He wants for me, He wants for you, too.

We are all in this thing together. He is not a respecter of persons (Acts 10:34, NIV). And if you live in a mansion, are more educated than me, and have a supermodel wife/husband, none of that makes you better than me in His eyes, only the world's. I know how He feels about me. I am very special in His eyes. And so are you, but it has nothing to do with your house, your money, or your job.

You can have your mansion and your relationship. But if you are without the fullness of Christ, compare my actions to yours and you will see who is fuller, even without a love relationship and money. I don't need anyone to tell me who I am. I don't always need people around me or some place to be. I don't need to drink, do drugs, smoke cigarettes, or make out with strangers in my spare time to entertain myself. I am at peace.

If only I recognized the lies that led me to believe I couldn't get that feeling we all felt when we were younger back. He wanted my heart so He could fix it. He loved me so much, I just had absolutely no idea.

I was never meant to feel negative feelings about myself. I was never meant to go through the hell that I have been through. But it happened. Rest assured, God's Holy Spirit can heal you, too if you need it. And He will if you only ask.

"If you remain in Me and My words remain in you, ask whatever you want and it will be done for you" (John 15:7 CSB).

I have every reason to hate sin. Sin is what came so close to destroying me. A bright, overpowering light drowned out the darkness and ultimately began the restoration of my soul.

Every moment is not blissful after committing or recommitting your life to the Lord. Life has its tough moments; however, you decide to live it and who you choose to live it for. Tough is inevitable. But even through your valleys, you will be at peace. And perfect peace is only the result of giving your life to the Lord.

It took me being convinced in a very powerful way, beyond any shadow of doubt that Satan could bring to my mind, that there is a power so magnificent and beautiful and worthy of my worship. That power came from God's Holy Spirit, the Father of Jesus Christ. I am convinced because I have proof. Where I am today is my own living proof.

Now is the time to step from the dark into the light. 'Cause you can't change what you've done, but you can choose who you'll become.

Partial lyrics to "Starting Over" by Addison Road

MY HEART

To love at all is to be vulnerable. Love anything and your heart will certainly be wrung and possibly broken.

C.S. Lewis, *The Four Loves*

GUARDING MY HEART

God can bless me with the most meaningful relationship I have ever experienced and have always desired. But if I'm not careful by guarding my heart and being protective of my mind, I can aid my flesh in the destruction of something beautiful. One example of not guarding my heart is when I allow myself to entertain thoughts that aren't in line with the present reality.

Entertaining my thoughts, such as fantasizing and daydreaming, can lead me to a place where I prematurely desire something from a relationship that it may or may not ever offer me. The truth is, what I desire sometimes may or may not ever be anything any person could ever completely fulfill within me, such as validation. Only God can fulfill that need. Besides, He is the best mirror anyway. The things He says about His children, no one could compete with those affirmations.

I've learned that when I place my fleshly expectations on the "imaginary" relationship, it can result in feelings of rejection, anxiety, and/or worry. Satan wants to keep us confused, anxious, and stressed out. What the flesh desires, you are either not meant to ever have, or at least not at this time. I try my best to keep the daydreaming under control.

When I told Mr. Harris about my daydreaming issues, he told me that it was natural that women do that because we were raised hearing of fairy tales and our "Prince Charming." So, once again, he ruled out the possibility that I was crazy.

THE DESIRES OF MY HEART

When we spend a lot of time in His presence, our hearts will naturally begin to seek His will. Pursuing righteousness is a side effect of spending time with Him in His Word, when you fellowship with other believers and when you praise Him as you sing along to your Christian music. That is what that is, praise and worship to your Maker, and He loves that.

They say we have two natures, our spirit and our flesh, and whichever you feed the most wins. That is why I don't listen to anything that would pull me down, whether it is music, television, movies, or the crowd I hang around. I want to only feed my spirit and starve my flesh if I want to successfully walk in His Spirit and in truth.

I believe when we are walking in the Spirit, rather than our flesh, we have a heart that seeks and lives to dwell in the presence of the Lord. And when you arrive at the place where you find your happiness in Him, He gives you the desires of your heart. It is a win-win situation. And according to Stephen Covey from *The Seven Habits of Highly Effective People*, we should strive for win-win scenarios.

"Delight yourself in the LORD and he will give you the desires of your heart" (Psalm 37:4, NIV).

Although the heart is deceitful above all things and it is not to be trusted, per Jeremiah 17:9, when your heart changes, so do your desires. What my heart desires now is completely different than what my heart desired years ago. I find myself attracted to guys for reasons I can't explain; it's something much deeper than appearance that draws me.

One time, I was so spiritually attracted to a guy that it didn't matter that he was a lot younger than me when I only date older guys. I was still drawn to the God I saw in him. I prayed that God would please have someone like him set aside for me. I knew my heart would be safe with someone who loved the Lord that much.

More recently, I was sitting in a waiting room chair, and a guy walked in the room. The moment I saw him, I jumped, and I immediately sat up straight. It was a reflex. I didn't think about it, and if I had I wouldn't have done that. It was so obvious and embarrassing.

Although I thought he was really cute, I believe it was more than that. After getting to know him, I discovered he had an amazing heart. In fact, probably the most attractive heart out of all the guys I have known. He had a heart that was not happy with sin. He had a heart for God.

And not only that, I also learned a lot from him. He encouraged my nature by telling me that I shouldn't change who I was to fit any sort of mold. My whole life I have felt that I needed to tone down who I was. It wasn't that he praised my nature, but he simply accepted me for who I was, which I have never had happen before by a male.

He also said sometimes God wants us to move first, which I took to heart. I believe it was an instant spiritual attraction for me. I believe the God in me, recognized the God in him. God also knew

I would need his friendship for a season and that our friendship would also aid in bringing me closer to the Lord. If for no other reason than that, I will always consider myself blessed for being given the opportunity to get to know him during that season in my life.

So that is why one verse in Jeremiah can say the heart is deceitful above all things and not to trust it, but then in Psalms it says that if we are delighting in Him, He will give us the desires of our heart. The Bible doesn't contradict itself. It only goes to show you that when we are abiding in Him, what we want will be in line with what He wants. In fact, I wouldn't put it past Him to have put the desires in our heart Himself when we are seeking Him.

BREAKUPS

It feels pretty good when you fully let someone in your heart. The connection is amazing. But what about when you decide to move on? In my experience, the pain can be excruciating. And even after it stops hurting and I have moved on, their memory resides in my heart forever.

I know in my deepest knowing they were all wrong for me. And I am so thankful that my prayers weren't fulfilled because they did not cherish me.

The deepest part of my being knows that they would've been a part of a life lived that was less for me than God's best. I would've settled. I would have sold myself short. I had more growing to do. I would not be the person I have become with them in my life, playing a part in holding me back from my destiny. When it comes to breakups, I would rather avoid them if I can. I have had enough.

A NEED TO BE VALIDATED

I lived a few years of my life where I was giving my heart away to those that didn't even want it, let alone ask for it. I was so driven to receive validation from the opposite sex. Even if it wasn't always consistent, there was always enough of it to keep me from facing reality. The reality was that I was alone, wounded, broken, and scared to death to feel the deep, dark, sickening feeling inside.

As with all my other self-medication techniques, I ultimately realized I was never doing myself a favor with covering up that feeling. A feeling that started with me feeling like an outcast as a child and only intensified over time from the negative feelings brought on by drug abuse, giving myself away, verbal abuse, the trauma from physical abuse, my chemically imbalanced new step dad calling me a "slut" when I was seventeen, and my dad handling me the way he was misled in doing so by not seeing me for six years from ages fifteen to twenty-one. All of that sent me the same message: I was defective and unworthy of love.

One of the main reasons I haven't opened up about my past is because of thoughts such as, *What will my future husband think?* and *Why would any good man want to marry me and my past if they knew the mistakes I've made?*

Even though most of the childhood pain that drove me to being bad wasn't my fault, who wants a heart with all these scars?

NO MORE SELLING MYSELF SHORT

Abstaining from sex before marriage is something I would do even if it wasn't a sin. If you are the type of person who enjoys exercise for the endorphin high, you would work out even if it didn't make you lose weight or affect your fitness level, right? Well I like the way purity feels. It took me awhile to feel it again. But I wouldn't trade it for anything.

Although I have been free from the bondage of sexual sin since 2006, I let it happen with my last boyfriend in October of 2007 by not speaking up for myself and saying no when I wanted to, and I cried as soon as it was over, but I made sure he didn't see. He later apologized because he knew I wasn't ready. The next day, all of my insecurities set in.

Because of my tendency toward preoccupied attachment, I looked at one of his social networking accounts without telling him. He had written a girl he was sleeping with prior to dating me a private message saying, "I know I shouldn't write you this, but you are so freaking sexy." Her response was along the lines of they needed to find some time to be able to "get together."

Reading those words crushed me. I am sure it was more devastating to me than most people because of my sensitive nature and triggers. But I also believe the hurt was more intense because I hadn't healed from all the past relationships yet. I would go from one relationship to the next, never having to get over any of them. They were all the same to me after the first one. And where that first one started wasn't even a boyfriend at all.

I had to leave work because it made me physically ill, the hurt was so intense. I felt betrayed, my pride was hurt, and I was hurt that the person I gave myself away to, when I knew better to do so, wasn't even satisfied with the most I could ever offer him. My family doesn't even know I slept with him.

The ending wasn't intense, and he wasn't crazy. I wasn't crazy by the time I met him; I just needed some more time to be single and heal. I had been on the path to healing and was on the right track. He knew a lot of my past, and maybe he did love me in the end as he claimed. We were just on two different paths spiritually, and that is okay. We still communicate in a friendly manner when we see each other. He has a girlfriend that he started dating shortly after we broke up. We both have moved on, and I wish him the best.

PURSUE GOD-CENTERED RELATIONSHIPS

Sometimes my mind asks myself, *Did I throw away a deep friendship love with someone in hopes of there being a better fit for me, when I might not ever even find it and end up alone?* My mom tells my girlfriends that I let go of a good one when referring to my last boyfriend of over three years ago. And if that ends up being the case, would I go back to what we had if I could? My answer is a tearful no.

I am not going to claim to be better than anyone. He had a beautiful heart. He would have been settling with me, and I would have been settling with him. You can't deny when you know you're settling with someone.

And if I end up being alone forever, that is okay. Because now that I am much further along in my healing, I am comfortable being alone. And I am at peace because I am not in a relationship that I know I shouldn't be in.

I choose peace, happiness, and a deeper relationship with Christ all by myself over being in a relationship with someone where Christ isn't at the center. I've read about those kinds of beautiful relationships, and I've seen them. That's what I want, and that is what I will not settle for less than.

I want someone who I can share my God discoveries with. I need more than a listener. I need someone who will understand them and have their own God discoveries to share with me, too.

No more unbelievers for me. I am no longer even interested in a lukewarm Christian. I want a man like Michael Hosea in *Redeeming Love* by Francine Rivers. He doesn't have to be loud and obnoxious about his faith, and I would prefer that he not be. But I want a man who has chosen a side. I want a man sold-out to Christ. Is that too much to ask?

LETTING GO

Even as far as guy friends go, letting go of people I have become close with emotionally has always been difficult since my ex-dad left my life. He was my protector while he was around. When he left, I was scared, and I didn't feel as safe. So if I feel safe and secure with someone enough to let my guard down, I naturally tend to become attached.

The only difference between me now and me back in the day is now I am more self-aware, and I have learned boundaries. I know one of my boundaries is the amount of time I communicate and the level I communicate. But when I get used to someone that feels safe in my life, I am still at the point where it hurts to let them go.

I haven't been in a relationship in nearly three years, which has been the best thing I could ever do to get well. I was clingy, emotional, dependent, and possessive with all of my boyfriends. None of that displays love, and all of that shows I was less than whole.

THE TOUGHEST

When I was living with my dad at fifteen, I met a boy. I had run away from home, and it was right after I started cutting. My self-esteem was shot at that time. He pursued me and showed interest, so that meant he had no chance with me. The only guys I was drawn to were the ones who didn't want me. The ones that did like me turned me off. I felt as if I had no value whatsoever and because they saw something of value, I felt something must be wrong with them.

The boy I met was actually a really good catch at the time, I just didn't know it. I confided in him, and we became friends. When he finally quit chasing me, he had my attention. I was a cheerleader and he played basketball at our school, and I remember when it happened—the moment God told me that he was good. I heard it in my heart and from that moment on, I held on to him.

I finally knew it was time to give him up in my heart this year, ten years later. He lived eight hundred miles away, and we hadn't even seen each other in four years. It was the last thing in my life separating me from God and His plans for my life. It was the only attachment in my life still causing me pain.

He started seeing someone on a more serious level, and it hurt. I had no business staying close to him when he had a girlfriend. My thoughts were that I was there first and that he must be "the one." He was the only thing from my past that didn't get destroyed in the wreckage. I was determined to hold on to him. But the pain of doing so, I soon realized, was going to cost me more than the pain of letting go.

Every time I would come to visit my dad but one time, he would lead me to believe we were going to hang out. And when we didn't,

I felt rejected on every level. But yet, I still held on. He was still someone more solid than myself who I could latch on to and feel safe emotionally. It is something I did in my heart at fifteen years old without his knowledge.

We had been close on-and-off since we were kids. I will always love him as a person. But he has no place in my future. And as I grow older, I realize who deserves to be close to me and who doesn't. God says my heart is precious, and He doesn't want it being broken over and over again.

There comes a point in your life when you realize who really matters, who never did, and who always will.

God told me he was good because he knew I would need him one day. When I was in the process of rebuilding from ground zero and putting my life back together, we reconnected. If it weren't for his friendship, I would not be where I am today. My last message to him was one of gratitude, the one where I finally let him go.

I told him in more or less words that I appreciated the ways in which he had been there for me in the past. I also told him no matter what he did, I would always think highly of him for that reason. I told him I wished him the very best. And I meant it.

It was the most painful of all my breakups, and it wasn't even a breakup. It was a break away from a friendship that deserved no explanation. It was a break away that left the unsaid, said through my silence because he knew me that well. He knew what I was saying in my last text message thanking him for his friendship, whether he believed it or not at the time. I believe he knew that was me saying good-bye for good.

My family never understood why I stayed friends with him because he never followed through. He was never a friend to me in their eyes. But he was more of a friend to me in other ways that no one but me could understand. One of my brothers, Chris, seemed to understand that some things you're not capable of understanding about other's relationships. He said that no one truly knows about a relationship unless they're one of the ones in it. God did me a favor by telling me he was good. And it worked in my favor that we lived far away, too, because we could never mess up our friendship that I needed during that time in life by ever hooking up.

I knew his heart, and I know how his friendship helped me when I simply needed a male to listen and talk to me. I didn't want a girl, I wanted a guy. He would always joke around, saying he felt like my dad. That's what it was really all about. And that is why I chose an older man as my counselor. I had a need for direction and advice from a man that needed to be met without any strings attached.

My childhood friend was a great person. He had never tried drugs or done the crazy things I had done. He was good, like He said. Because he was good, I knew I had to be good, too, for him to like me. He helped me be better, and he didn't even know it. He raised my standards for guys. Was he sold out and on fire for God? If he wasn't, I pray he will be.

That boy and now grown man doesn't know any bit of my story. I kept it from him because I felt he wouldn't be my friend if he knew. And because of that, I will never know the truth. I will never know if he was ever truly my friend. And I am perfectly fine leaving the unsaid, in this case, unsaid.

MARRIAGE

I have heard it said that you can never be 100 percent sure about anything, including the decision to marry your husband or wife. I disagree. When God is at the center and you allow Him to coordinate the events to line up with His will, plan, and purposes for your life, we will never be sure of anything more.

You know those divine appointments? You can just feel that God just did something special and you were a part of it. He literally came down and spoke to us, we heard, we acted, we met, we talked, we learned, we were healed and/or encouraged, we felt His presence, and we left forever changed and connected to the other person and their soul. We will recognize them in heaven whether we ever see them again on earth.

I feel like you can't deny something like that. You felt it. You saw it. You were there. I know that is what the love story of my life that God can give me can be like if I step out of the way. I just have to stop analyzing and worrying about something that will never come about the way I want if I am in charge.

I have to place the end result in His hands and follow His lead for what He wants for me right now according to His will, plan, and purposes for my life. The future is in His hands, just like the present, if I submit. My life couldn't be placed in any better care. So I need to give it up. I can rest assured that I don't have to control this one.

MY FUTURE

Even though I go through moments of doubt that I won't ever be emotionally healthy enough to attract the kind of winner my heart desires, I have to believe in His promises. They've gotten me this far.

I claim right now, in Jesus' name, that I will have a family one day. I will love from a whole, all the pieces of my heart put back together place, and I will let myself feel his love. Why? Because my God says I am deserving of love.

The relationship with my future husband will be healthy. We will be equally yolked. Our marriage will be centered in God. My husband will be my family's spiritual leader. He will love my daughter, and the love I see him showing her will bring me even more healing. I can envision it now.

And his love will feel so safe. He won't ever make me feel scared. He will never verbally or physically abuse me. He will be protective of me. And I will not be preoccupied with his whereabouts and him cheating on me. We will be united as one, with God being first in our lives. I will be first in his life and he will be first in mine, with God being first between us. Picture a triangle where God is at the top and you and your significant other are side by side at the bottom. We will both pursue righteousness and God together.

We will inspire each other.

He will love my heart. And because I will let him see all of it, his love for me will be even that much more tender. I will be cherished. And my heart will be pursued before I give it to him. He won't bring up my past in fights. He will love me as a friend first. For love is friendship set on fire. I will be his sister, his lover, and his bride.

I will have my first wedding that I never knew I deserved. My dad will walk me down the aisle. And God will be the designer of it all. Because all of the desires in this heart of mine, He placed inside.

> *"To fall in love is easy. But it is a hard quest worth making to find a comrade through whose steady presence one becomes steadily the person one desires to be."*
>
> Anna Louise Strong

LOVING MYSELF

The entire law is summed up in a single command: "Love your neighbor as yourself."

Galatians 5:14 (NIV)

That verse is one of the Ten Commandments. We are commanded to love our neighbors as ourselves because it is assumed that we love ourselves. If I truly love myself, I won't put up with others mistreating me. And I won't mistreat myself either.

How can I criticize our King of king's creation and think He is all right with that? He says for me to stop the obsession with self and perfection. Only He is perfect. It is the enemy that drives me to perfection. It is a never-ending battle, and it will not be won.

When I cut or starved myself, I was not being loving. I didn't show love to my body when I didn't make exercise a priority to keep my heart healthy. And when I was consuming drugs and cigarettes, I was saying to my health, "I don't care what these toxins do to you. I do what I feel regardless of how it affects you."

I wasn't taking care of my liver when I drank alcohol in excess. That's not love. And when I still stand in the mirror only to scrutinize and pick my body apart to this day, I am rejecting myself.

> *"I may give away everything I have, and I may even give my body as an offering to be burned. But I gain nothing if I do not have love. Love is patient and kind. Love is not jealous, it does not brag, and it is not proud. Love is not rude, is not selfish, and does not get upset with others. Love does not count up wrongs that have been done. Love*

is not happy with evil but is happy with the truth. Love patiently accepts all things. It always trusts, always hopes, and always remains strong. Love never ends."

1 Corinthians 13:3-9, NCV

PERFECTIONISM

I started picking myself a part at twelve-years-old. Even before I was twelve, I would sit in the sink and stare at my few freckles around my nose with disgust. And that was before acne. Boy, I was in for a real treat. My mom told me when I was a little girl that if my freckles still bothered me that she would pay to have them removed when I got married. Freckles are the least of my worries now.

Now if you could just take away my cellulite, remove the excess fat here, here, and there. Erase the scars on my face that my compulsive picking left me with. Give me calf implants and bigger boobs. I love my hair as long as I don't see another gray. And while we're at it, you can miraculously make me weigh ten pounds less, since I identify with that number so much. I don't even care if I look ten pounds less as much as I care that the stupid number goes down on the scale. You can feel free to trick me, but don't ever tell me. As long as the number goes down, I will feel satisfied because I will feel in control. And God knows I like it when I am in control.

Look, I am going to tell you the truth. Satan knows how to get to us. That's what all of this self-hatred, body image, and perfectionism is about.

I LOVE YOU

I come up with these little exercises sometimes to help me grow. What helped me grow in love toward myself was a friend telling me about her "crazy" mother suggesting she say "I love you" in the mirror to make herself feel better. As soon as we got off the phone, I headed for the bathroom.

I told myself "I love you" for the first time in the mirror in June of 2009. I looked myself in the eyes, said those words, and lost it. Needless to say, it meant something to me to have that kind of effect. All the things I have done to my body and have put up with over the years made me feel neglected. I was telling myself I hated myself on a daily basis through my actions.

Since I knew that worked, I wrote a message to myself that I said in the mirror every day in addition to the "I love you." Now, I just look at it occasionally. I keep it in my purse as a reminder. I don't need to constantly affirm myself because that need to feel loved by myself was finally met after many days of reciting my little love letter written to me.

Here is what my letter said that I would recite while looking myself in the eyes, don't forget that part.

I love you. I respect you. You are brilliant. You are a genius. I have confidence in you because you are confident and secure with yourself and will not settle for less than the best in men, relationships, work and life. The sky is the limit when you stay true to you! You're beautiful and your future is bright! This moment is exactly as it should be. You are perfect the way you are. But there is always room for improvement. If you're not learning you're dying. Live life to the fullest and treasure each moment as if it were a gift from God, because it is!

The God that gave me my life back is the One who represents love in its purest, and for me since I like intense, most intense form. He wants me to love myself. Talk about making a girl fall in love over a weekend. Wow.

Part of loving myself also involves being able to be happy by myself. I will say when I first started making myself spend time alone, I would feel that uncomfortable feeling rise up. But you know what? The more I exercised that hole by getting by myself, the stronger I got.

I have been known to force myself to do things just to conquer the fear. When I bought my first movie ticket to watch by myself, I thought in the back of my head, *She is thinking I am such a loser right now. Who goes to the movies alone? Everyone is going to think I don't have any friends. If I run into someone I know, should I go ahead and tell them this is just an "exercise" and that is the only reason I am by myself?* Then when I got in to the theater, I thought, *Wow, no one even cares. No one is paying me any attention or looking in my direction.* The first time was a trip, but I got used to it.

SHAME

> *"Those who look to him are radiant; their faces are never covered with shame."*
>
> Psalm 34:5, NIV

When we don't forgive ourselves for our past, the shame sets in. I am not proud of the drugs, but I have dealt with more shame over my past sexual sin than I have over anything else.

I know what it feels like when you are being used. I also know what it feels like to be so accustomed to the feeling that I didn't even know I was worthy of anything more. I didn't know turning around was an option. I didn't know that I didn't have to feel that way. I didn't know I deserved better.

I grew accustomed to the feeling. It was familiar, and I was comfortable. Over time, feeling used felt natural to me. I was playing a role that none of us, male or female, should've ever learned to play.

FORGIVING MYSELF

Remorse is a beautiful thing because it is evidence that God is in control. The things I could once do without regret now pains my heart that it happened.

Do you want to know what God told my heart about my shame when I came to Him crying? He said to my heart:

> *I do not care what you did or who you did it with. I already knew about it when it was going on. I know every deep dark secret that no one else knows, and I found you worthy enough to still pursue you. Why? Because it doesn't matter to me. I see you for who you are, not the things you were once doing.*
>
> *My precious child, I know you better than you know yourself. No man, woman, father, mother, brother, aunt, or friend could ever love you more than me. And my love is all you truly need to make you happy. Just wait. You will see.*
>
> Love,
> Your heavenly Father

THE TRINITY

"Praise be to the God and Father of our Lord Jesus Christ, the Father of compassion and the God of all comfort."

2 Corinthians 1:3, NIV

Unfortunately, I can't sit here pure and righteous with this clean and perfect past. God redeemed me. I think that is pretty obvious; my past is crazy. Unbelievable, even. God has truly done a work in me.

INTERCESSORY PRAYER

My love for the hurting is so strong because I know I have felt at least something they have felt that hurts. I don't care who you are or what you're involved in. If you're hurting, I feel your pain.

When I pray for people, sometimes I feel this heaviness come over me. When I first noticed it happen was when I was at this special church service about a year ago, and I was praying for one of my younger sisters. As I begged God in my heart for her to not go through the things I have and suffer from low self-esteem, I started crying, and this heaviness came on me that made me lose my balance.

What I am trying to say is that when I intercede in prayer, not only do I "feel your pain," I actually do "feel" it. I think that is why I am so set out on writing this book after God gave me the "invisible audience." I really do love others so much. It's just loving myself that is the fighting battle.

There is an accessible power that comes down to those whose hearts plead for it. It heals, reveals, changes, restores, and cleanses. That presence is the Lord's. Don't be deceived; there is a spiritual realm. And His Holy Spirit reigns.

And the dark side, if you really knew what it consisted of, you would think twice before you knowingly sinned.

JESUS

The more you pursue God, the closer you will get to fully experiencing Him. We know of our Creator Father and His Son, Jesus Christ. He is our example as Christians, not to mention the one who paid a price for us He didn't even owe. He gave the ultimate sacrifice for us. And He did it because He knew we needed it.

Who would you die for? Someone you dearly love? What about someone you've never even met, but you know that there is something beyond this place so whether you've met them or not, you love their soul? Jesus saw the big picture.

Jesus was an example of what we could be and proved it could be done. Sin does not have to be a part of our everyday lives. We do not have to use the grace card all the time. I do it through my impatience, my disrespect for my mother at times, being messy, and my aggressive driving skills, to name a few. I am far from perfect. But I know He is displeased when people don't acknowledge their faults and earnestly work at being more like Jesus. So for that reason, I will always be a work in progress, because I will never stop trying.

GOD

God is pleased when we do our best. And for me, my best today looks nothing like what my best was years ago. He understands that when breaking addictions, unless you have some kind of supernatural experience where He delivers you of everything at once, it will take time. He understands that you may fall and how easy it is for you to do so.

But at the same time, He reads our hearts. If your heart is to please Him and you repeatedly fall, you will eventually get it right. I finally did after many years of stumbling. At least it didn't take me forty years in the desert like it did the Israelites. I always kept that story in the back of my mind and only prayed that it wouldn't take me that long to reach the Promised Land, the land I find myself in today.

God has compassion on His children. I relapsed time and time again. I was a lot like David, the boy who killed the giant, Goliath. David was someone who got himself in a lot of trouble. He had sex outside of marriage with another man's wife. She became pregnant, and he tried to cover his trouble by making an even bigger mess. It was pretty dramatic.

In the end, David repented and his heart was deeply troubled, not because he sinned against man, but because he sinned against God. David was a man after God's own heart. And God blessed him for that.

THE HOLY SPIRIT

> *"Now, it happened that while Apollos was away in Corinth, Paul made his way down through the mountains, came to Ephesus, and happened on some disciples there. The first thing he said was, "Did you receive the Holy Spirit when you believed? Did you take God into your mind only, or did you also embrace him with your heart? Did he get inside*

you?" "We've never even heard of that— a Holy Spirit? God within us?" "How were you baptized, then?" asked Paul. "In John's baptism." "That explains it," said Paul. "John preached a baptism of radical life-change so that people would be ready to receive the One coming after him, who turned out to be Jesus. If you've been baptized in John's baptism, you're ready now for the real thing, for Jesus." And they were. As soon as they heard of it, they were baptized in the name of the Master Jesus. Paul put his hands on their heads and the Holy Spirit entered them. From that moment on, they were praising God in tongues and talking about God's actions. Altogether there were about twelve people there that day."

Acts 19: 1-7, The Message

Why does it seem that there are many Christians in the world today who have forgotten about the third head of the Trinity, the Holy Spirit? The Holy Spirit is part of the Trinity that is acknowledged by every denomination that I personally consider Christian. The Holy Spirit is the only tangible part of God. It plainly states the power of the Holy Spirit in the Holy Bible, in every version. Why do some people get uncomfortable with Him?

If you love me, you must love my heart, my mind, and my soul. If you reject any part of who I am, you may have access to my heart because I am loving—but you will never experience all that I have to offer you as a person. Do you read your bible? Okay, good. Because if you do, then I am going to go ahead and assume you don't freak out about the mention of or the manifestations of God's Holy Spirit. One of Webster's definitions of blasphemy is: irreverent behavior toward anything held sacred, priceless, etc.

"And so I tell you, every sin and blasphemy will be forgiven men, but the blasphemy against the Spirit will not be forgiven" (Matthew 12:31, NIV).

Ignorance in this case is not bliss. Pretty sure that if you are a follower of Christ's teachings, you shouldn't put it past a God that created a universe and sent His spotless Lamb whose presence is here to teach, guide, and counsel us to not be powerful enough to make Himself known on earth in a godlike fashion.

THE HOLY SPIRIT BAPTISM VS. THE KUNDALINI AWAKENING

Before I tell you about my experience with God's Holy Spirit, I wanted to share some information with you about the demonic stuff that is going on out there imitating God's Holy Spirit, so you don't fall prey to its lures.

I am going to start off with the "Kundalini awakening." The result of having this Kundalini spirit "activated" or transmitted to the person is that the spirit enters and starts the "activation" in your spine and works its way up, "lighting up the chakras." The whole experience is enticing when you hear about the healing, visions, and demonic spiritual gifts such as psychic abilities that can come from it. But what you don't hear is that it is the counterfeit of God's Holy Spirit baptism, oftentimes even being called the Holy Spirit's baptism to add to its further deception.

God's Holy Spirit brings you healing, and you don't have to experience severe body contortions resulting in excruciating pain and uncomfortable muscle spasms that leave you sore and bruised. I have read stories of where the inhibitor of the demonic spirit's body will start jerking in the middle of the night violently and uncontrollably. But they are being purged from some things during the process that brings them some healing. So they put up with it, thinking that the "Lord" is having them suffer for due cause, when that is not my precious Lord Jesus at all; that is quite the opposite. If they only knew God's means of healing doesn't cause them any pain whatsoever.

Some believe that the "Kundalini" is already in each of us and that it only needs to be "activated." The truth is this spirit is not in them unless it is transmitted via the laying on of hands by someone with spirit in them or in some cases through reciting something the pastor instructs through the television set.

This infiltration of the counterfeit Holy Spirit does everything God's does such as healing, visions, and speaking in tongues, but with a demonic twist. Satan's version of the gift of tongues makes you bark like a dog and/or roar like a lion. Demonic much? I think so. On top of that, the spirit's oppression ultimately leads to one's possession if it isn't cast out. After all, wouldn't that be Satan's goal—to steal your soul from God?

I would say a full-blown possession has taken place as opposed to partial possession or oppression when the leaders of churches are encouraging others to partake from the "tree of life," but it is clearly not the tree of life, just like it isn't Jesus they are claiming to see and talk to. These folks are also embracing the opening of their "third eye," which I can tell you from experience is demonic, and it isn't any "gift" I want any part in. That detailed account is in my next book, and it is trippy.

Some pastors that are involved are not only verbally admitting to and encouraging the use of their third eye; they are physically exhibiting the eye in the form of a tattoo on their arm. That would be one of the same pastors who is baptizing people in the Kundalini spirit but calling it the "Holy Spirit" to woo Christians.

Yes, those possessed by the Kundalini spirit feel bliss and higher than crack during the "activation." I am sure they even feel all powerful with their knowledge and enlightenment, but their souls and their hearts are filthy. Therefore, they still feel dejected. Only God, the Creator of their souls, can clean up the mess that sin has brought upon them. The Kundalini awakening purges you to some degree, but it can't do that.

I believe there are those out there who truly believe God is behind their new enlightenment. And of those "deceived," some are leading their congregation and spreading this demonic spirit revival, all the while maintaining an admitted adulterous affair. How innocently deceived do you think the latter's hearts could be? And who do you think is going to be judged more, the leaders or the followers? It would be the ones who are leading their flock astray.

God's Holy Spirit isn't going to make you bark like a dog. Stay in the Word and use common sense. I am not gently presenting this issue because it is a major deception going on to some people who truly have a heart for God but were just deceived, and it is quite offensive. Call this righteous indignation, and if I had something to throw or overturn to get people's attention like Jesus did when they were selling animals to be sacrificed in the outer courts of the temple, I would. That spirit needs to be cast out immediately. That is not a part of my ministry at this time, but I have some contacts that can help you if you are one of the ones who were innocently deceived.

And don't be enticed by the third eye, either. You will go insane just like you hear the people talking on YouTube who catch demons in jars when they go to bed at night because they can visually see them. Seriously, even in my wildest days, I would've never been enticed by that.

God has been giving Christians visions and prophecies since time began. Satan is stirring things up with his obvious imitations, such as the "third eye" and that Kundalini spirit. They have to achieve physical pain only to receive a fraction of the peace, enlightenment, and fulfillment that God's Holy Spirit brings an individual.

Bottom line, do not let just anyone lay hands on you to pray in this "New Age" and day. Satan's biggest and most powerful weapon is little ole' deception, and he is winning some of the oldest, most well-known pastors with all the Eastern mysticism and "Christian New Age" infiltrating the church. Go to the Internet and do some research on the "Kundalini awakening" for further information.

As far as when I was baptized by God's sovereign Holy Spirit, I didn't even need any assistance or laying on of hands. I was with my mother at a worship service. It was less than a year after the "door incident." My heart was not over the man who did that to me. But after I left that night, it was well on its way.

The second time of His many outpourings to come, I was delivered from a lot of shame from my past that I had been dealing with. The lady that prayed over me was Robin Gilliam, Pastor Jerry's wife from New Beginnings Church. She said that God said I was "pure as the driven snow." As I cried that shame out of me, I had never felt a release from crying at that intensity before. It was almost as if He opened the flood gates and pushed it out of me. My precious God wanted me delivered from shame so I could one day be where I am today, writing you.

I had actually been abstinent for a few years at the time of that second outpouring of His Holy Spirit. However, the reflection I saw in the mirror was someone who was dirty. I saw a girl who had done things she was not proud to admit, even to herself. Although I knew God had His hand on my life and that I was His, the verse in Acts saying that Jesus washed away my sins wasn't enough to actually make me feel pure. My mind had wrapped around the concept, but my soul needed His actual cleansing.

The Bible says that Jesus washes our sins away (Acts 22:16). Well after that second outpouring, I believe He did. The very next day when I looked at myself in the mirror, I felt as if a veil had been lifted off to reveal the person underneath all the muck.

Eventually, my supernatural encounters with God's Holy Spirit would be so intense during praise and worship all by myself that asking Him to purge me of all my impurities and past iniquities wasn't necessary. His presence overwhelmed me and flooded out the darkness still inside of me through my tears and sobs that I would experience in our time together.

Personally, I didn't have to seek out any form of deliverance; He took care of me without me even knowing that I was being delivered. All I knew was that the tears made me feel better.

DRAW NEAR TO GOD

The more we draw near, the more we are like Him. Personally, I had to pray for God to put a desire to pursue Him in my heart. Prayer closets, morning devotionals, and being on fire for God didn't sound like any fun at all. Ask for the desire, and He will gladly fulfill the request.

I finally said, "Lord, I want what you want me to have. Make me desire to love you how you want."

God gives presents. He gives gifts that make us think, *What does He see in me? Why am I so special? Does He not know everywhere I have been? Does He not realize I had four shots of tequila this past New Year's Eve before selling out to Him completely?*

If you are one of the many who believe that the gifts of the Spirit such as tongues, healing, visions, prophesying, and many more are only meant for the time of Pentecost in the book of Acts, you are deceived. I don't speak in tongues, but I don't talk against it. You can't argue with experience or Jesus. You may not have all of the gifts. But they are gifts I know He wants to give us. Press in to Him and check out Francis Chan's *Forgotten God* for some more insight on the Holy Spirit.

HIS CALLING

His calling has always been so intense on my life. Whether on acid, working as a bartender, or being drunk on New Year's Eve 2010, He has never hesitated to seek connection with me.

This past New Year's Eve, I found myself in a predicament. I was out with a guy that apparently had a fiancée a week before. I knew he had broken up with his girlfriend, but I didn't know how serious they were. I talked to her before I went out with him and assured her I was only his date to the event, and I would let him know as soon as we met up that it would be nothing past that.

But when we went out, he was one of those charmers. And I hadn't been on many dates in the past few years. Plus, I still had a weak area for male attention. Although I would never fall for a guy overly showering me with attention, I soaked it up that night.

However, in the back of my mind, I felt so guilty because of his ex-fiancée. I couldn't dance because I felt uptight. My conscience was killing me, but I felt stuck. The truth is I should have gone home the moment I felt uncomfortable being with a guy I wasn't truly interested in, who had an ex-fiancée who was a really sweet girl. But the thought of going home to spend my second New Year's Eve in a row by myself was depressing.

Our group went to the Chattanooga Trade and Convention Center to a party. To loosen up, I took four back-to-back shots of tequila. That was actually me being somewhat in control. I got up from my date at our table because I thought I saw my friend who had disappeared for a while with her boyfriend. When I got out to the lobby, I didn't see her anywhere in any direction.

At that point, I decided to walk outside by myself to be alone for a few minutes and get a breath of fresh air. On the way outside, I noticed there were these teenagers praying in the lobby to my left. As I passed them to go outside, I told God, "Do not call me out." But deep down, I secretly wanted Him to. I never admitted that even to myself until just now.

When I walked back inside, there was this other drunkard telling that same group that speaking in tongues without an interpreter was unbiblical. There was a Christmas tree in the middle of the lobby, so I decided to stand behind it and eavesdrop.

The poor little group of kids and one mother were not winning the battle against the drunken guy. He was overpowering them. I wasn't hearing any scriptures referenced to defend themselves; they were too drunk in the Spirit, if you ask me.

I know I have this boldness within me that comes out at times. I am not one to be over-powered in the way he was doing them. Plus, I am a need-meeter; I see a need, I meet it. I have to stop myself from always meeting other's needs when I see it. If I allow someone to depend on me, I am getting in His way. He wants them depending on Him, not me.

As I was eavesdropping behind the Christmas tree, part of me was saying to go back into the party and avoid the confrontation, but the other part of me won. I walked out from hiding and went straight up to him and told him he was wrong. I told him they were speaking with tongues and that was their prayer language, which didn't need an interpreter. The drunken guy ended up leaving them alone after asking me if I had a cigarette.

Then, Karine Cherry (the mother of one of the girls) approached me and asked, "Are you called to preach? I think you are." I told her that I didn't think I was. She also told me that even though I was drunk, God spoke to her heart as I approached them, "Honor her."

Then her daughter, Karissa Cherry, walked up to me and asked me what my name was, and I told her. At that time, she started crying. I could sense she was under the influence of the Holy Spirit because I had my first experience a year prior. I thought, *Uh-oh.* Then she asked my last name. When I told her, she said, "Oh my gosh, I can't believe this is her."

A few weeks prior, God gave her this dream that when she came to Chattanooga, there was a girl she was supposed to meet. Apparently, I was the mystery girl. In her dream, she had long brown hair with curls. Her name started with a C, and her last name was Italian. She and her mom even started searching on the Internet to find me.

She told me these very personal inner things I had been dealing with such as feelings of shame and my obsession with the number on the scale. She told me that God wanted me to know that He thought I was lovely and beautiful. Lovely was a first for me, and I got emotional at that point because of that, and because I was drunk.

What she was saying, as far as all the things He felt about me, was speaking straight to my heart and soul. I know it was God's Spirit telling me through her. It was a reminder to me that He wasn't letting go of me and that He viewed me as special. I have been different ever since that night. I have never felt so sought after.

Karissa and I departed after my friends showed up. My date handled it better than any of my other past boyfriends would have. My friends were as understanding as people can be who haven't experience the Holy Spirit's ways. Karissa left me with a note that read:

New Life Bible College

Cleveland, Tn-Norvel Hayes Ministries- Jan 6th 2nd semester starts

You are so welcome to come! Even if to sit in the classes for no cost. God wants your heart and he loves you with EVERY thing! Don't be scared of the things He has for you, cause they are far more wonderful than you can imagine! Don't let anyone (even yourself!) talk down to you or make you think you're crazy, this has happened for a reason! Don't deny God calling you! He loves your heart and wants to show you his =)

-Karissa Cherry (look me up on Facebook!)
Jesus loves you and so do I!-I'm still praying for you.

HOW HE PURSUED MY HEART AND WON

A woman's heart should be so lost in God's that a man has to seek Him just to find hers.

Maya Angelou

THE FAVORITE

I grew up in a furniture store pretty much. Before it became successful, there wasn't a lot of furniture, and it was a large building. For a while I was allowed to drive my Barbie car around it. Then that had to stop for the customers as the business grew. I would play by myself all the time because all my siblings were at least five years younger than me.

One day, I stopped at one of the dresser and mirror sets. I remember I propped my elbows on the dresser and sat my face in my hands while smiling at myself in the mirror. I wasn't criticizing what was wrong with me or my appearance. I was simply pleased with what I saw. I smiled at myself joyfully. I wasn't thinking I was pretty or practically perfect in every way, I believe I was simply seeing myself through His eyes, the same eyes I see myself through now.

That time at the dresser/mirror set was the time I could've swore God told me I was His favorite. Funny, I can still see my face in my hands in the mirror. I was wearing something light blue, probably a dress with jellies. I guess He knew that memory of would be an inspiration to us all now, especially me.

HE'S THERE FOR ME

I didn't believe that God was really there before recently. I thought there was a chance this was all in everyone's head. I didn't believe that God could ever meet my emotional needs. I also had pain that I needed to go away, and I couldn't give Him time with it just being us for Him to heal it. Now I know that I had God there this whole time. And if I had given Him more time or simply asked, He would've come through for me sooner.

I don't ever have to feel like I am alone anymore. He knew what He was doing to me. He knew He could outdo the rest, and I would be impressed. He knew I would appreciate the effort that was involved to win me over.

For a girl who has thrown her heart out there time and time again, as if it were worth absolutely no value whatsoever, having my heart pursued to the extent in which He did makes me cry. Everything He does makes me cry.

I've never felt this love; that's why it melts my heart, because of the way His love and obvious pursuit makes me feel on the inside. Why would I ever settle with any man who would hurt me ever again? He knew how the effort alone would make me feel. No one I have cared for has ever pursued me with pure intentions. He found the way to my heart. For that, my heart is forever His.

CONNECTION

I am not going to compare myself to Moses, but I wonder how he felt after seeing God? All I did was yield to where I was feeling led, and it put me in a three-day trance where I felt so connected with Him. I didn't want to interrupt any of it.

I didn't realize it at the time, but He was speaking to my heart through the impressions I thought were for you. I would have my eyes closed, crying as I poured my heart out to you because I knew you needed it during those impressions. After I read over it, I saw where I would say things like, "You will have a family, once you are well," and "You will be healed."

The reason those intense impressions happened was because I had just went in to what I was calling "the throne room of God" to pray. It was really my little sister's bedroom. I was probably going in her room instead of mine because mine was a wreck. I am not sure why her room got to be throne room that weekend, but it did.

Let's not forget I was tripping on Jesus at this time, so I have an excuse for being out of this world. Well, as I was praying and crying my heart out to Him to "please just reveal your heart to the reader" because I felt you needed it, I got to see His heart, too.

HE MAKES ME FEEL SPECIAL

I like to feel special. I like being people's favorite, whether it is the teacher's pet to the girl the guy picked. I like to feel important. So He knew what to do since He knows me better than any other.

He met my need and blew my mind. Yes, I did come back to earth. But He brought me back with a vision. I came back with a mission. The purpose He planted in my heart instantaneously brought the career fulfillment I had been seeking.

It didn't take much convincing for me as a child. I am not saying everyone will experience Him in the same way. He just did what He needed to do to mend His daughter's heart and make her feel loved. It took a whole lot of power and love with this heart. His love also healed my mind. His light drowned out the dark parts of my story.

He left me with a heavenly perspective that has changed my view on this vapor of a life. I was as close to heaven on earth as I have ever been. He knew I would talk about it too, because he knows I like to talk. I believe He gave me something special because He knew I would glorify Him with it. He knew He could trust me. And sweetest of all, He knew this heart needed it.

I needed to feel special. I needed to feel full so I would stop seeking affirmation elsewhere. I was seeking affirmation from everyone but Him. I sought it from my dad, my stepmom, my mother, my cousins, my aunts, my siblings, my crushes, and from anyone whose positive thoughts about me could assist in filling me up for the moment. And this was even after I recovered.

All the times He has called me out, the ways in which He has led people to tell me I was on His mind, He did that because He knew I would like that. He knew once I let Him all the way back in, I would see it. And that would move me incredibly because no one has ever pursued me in that way. I truly do get to see my worth through my Maker's eyes. And so can you. He is big enough to make us all feel special.

HE MAKES ME FEEL HEALTHY

My experience led to the fullness of Christ. I would rather be happy, healthy and whole as opposed to killing myself with the drugs and wasted living. Wouldn't you rather be happy, healthy, and whole, too?

What if it meant you had to go through something pretty supernatural to fix you once and for all? Would you place limits and demands on Him, such as, "God, I will do this only if you don't do this and you do that"? Would you let your fear of what people would think of you stop you from pursuing Him? If so, you will never have what I have.

HE FILLS ME

I lost the desire to attach to others when I fell in love with God. He filled me up once and for all. Not one bit of me is missing a piece anymore. I am more than whole; I am overflowing. I can spend on others and not expect anything from them.

> *"When you taste a measure of being able to love and enjoy the people in your life, without having to have any particular response from them, you are tasting bliss."*
>
> Paula Rinehart

You put two halves of a person together, and it is not like basic math. They do not equal a whole. And when you pull the two halves apart, there is less than the half of a piece of the person you began with, still unlike basic math. You feel emptier than you were before you met them.

God only gives to me. What could I do for Him? Simply praise Him and be obedient is all. I haven't sung my heart out and raised my hands to people. But when all I can do is think about another person and how I can please them, they replace God. They become an idol.

I don't have to worship Him, but I do. We have this innate desire to worship. I would worship guys who did not deserve to be worshipped. Even if it is the man God has set aside for me, he wouldn't deserve it, either. God is the One I was created to worship. And that is why the desire to worship is in my heart.

Reckless abandonment to His will is beautiful. Now I don't have to sit at home to keep me from sinning. I can have a drink and not have the compulsion to have more and end up drunk. The desire is just not there. I am full on God.

Would I risk replacing His fullness with a temporary high that would leave me emptier than when I started? I don't think so. Besides, if I knowingly sin without repentance, how will I hear Him like I do now? It would separate us. The "noise" would keep me from hearing His heart, because sin separates you from God.

HE PROTECTS ME

Until I have an earthly husband protecting and loving me, I have His protection. And now I can see why singers like Misty Edwards don't feel called to marriage and why many others aren't, either. I can see why in heaven, there wouldn't be any marriages.

It's almost scary to think I would have to give up some of my time with Him for a husband and children one day. Would He be there just as much? In my other relationships, I always had to choose between the two. God never won back then.

There is absolutely nothing in me driving me to pursue or even strategically be in the right place at the right time for anyone. That's how it is supposed to be anyway. Women are supposed to be pursued.

Just like God pursued my heart, no one else should have it without doing so. No more giving it away to the undeserving, only for it to be disregarded and trampled upon. Finally those days are over. He is protecting my heart until then.

HE ACCEPTS ME JUST AS I AM

He wanted to not only make me fill full for the weekend; He wanted to continually demonstrate His love by keeping me that way. How amazing is that? Cocaine was never my friend. When I came down from God's high, I was left overflowing and radiating, rather than empty and destitute. I believe that He wanted to show me the fullness of Christ. He wanted to show me that He could do what Satan did, but better.

Don't forget, Satan imitates. God creates.

Some may feel that my "weekend getaway" was a bit radical, to say the least. You know, I couldn't agree with you more. I have heard of wilder though. Whether you know what kind of high that first line of cocaine can bring you or not, just believe me when I say He made me higher in my heart. He knew how to get my attention. I am forever hooked on Him, and He knows it.

If you have never known what emptiness feels like or that sick feeling in your stomach that makes you wish death upon yourself, then it may not make sense how an experience such as mine could change the course of my entire life. However, if you have an IQ and the ability to analyze, maybe you can still catch on. Bottom line, He gave me the opposite of empty. Just know He meets you where you are, specific to your needs. And He doesn't love me more than He loves you.

HIS LOVE SPELL

If God wanted to keep me in my house and communicate with me at that level of intensity for the rest of my life, I wouldn't have walked away. But in the back of my mind, I knew I still had clothes in my closet with tags on them that I was looking forward to wearing. And there were just other responsibilities and obligations that would cause for the ending. I didn't get too attached to the high, but I did to God.

The spell was amazing, but I knew I couldn't stay there. He gave me a taste of heaven, but I have a job to do while I am still here. We are all called to help direct the lost to where they need to go. Why do we fail Him in that area? What are we so scared of? I know the answer and so do you. We are scared of what the rest of the world will think.

Although I came down, I didn't have to spend all day in bed recuperating with a roll of toilet paper. And I didn't have a tidal wave of anxiety and panic come upon me when I realized it was time for it to end. There wasn't any sort of unhealthy attachment going on, and He didn't make me feel abandoned when it was over.

My thoughts were that I was glad it happened because now I truly believed. As a true believer, I could then be an effective Christ follower and begin witnessing for the first time in my life. The idea was starting to become appealing to me. I finally understood how the Christian singers were so into their love songs to God. There is no more doubt in this mind.

HE PUT MY BROKEN PIECES TOGETHER

He set me free from the shame of my past by giving me His perspective. He gave me a vision of how my past would be used for His purpose. That is one of the most meaningful parts of that experience. I was given a gift for something I had hated about myself. I was given a purpose for something that had made no sense in my mind for having happened—my crazy past.

The secrets I had kept hidden had not only been weighing me down, they had also been holding me back from my destiny. My past is not beautiful, but He told me He could put the pieces together and that my story would be part of His plan. Now that the whole story is put together, I see the beauty too.

The following week, these messages kept coming to my head. I was scared to not jot down every single one of them. What if they never came back? Good thing I like intense. I didn't want to ask Him to tone it down because I enjoyed it. It was my evidence that what happened was real. It wasn't just my imagination.

HE LEADS ME

He gave me a new piece of the puzzle each day. I loved the mystery. One day, I hadn't received my new piece, and it was almost 2 p.m. I got in the elevator and said in my heart, *Well?* in a way that was expecting Him to come through. I didn't feel comfortable leading any bit of this. I didn't want it to turn into "my" thing, because then I wouldn't trust it. This was His thing. And I trusted Him.

It hit me after receiving my latest puzzle piece that if I had multiple books come out at one time, it might be noticeable and a bit of a big deal to the rest of the world. How would I handle it if, by chance, the whole world knew I as a former bad girl?

I know God isn't going to give me something I can't handle. I am both excited and scared. It is the good kind of scared. It is the kind of scared that says, "Things are going to be better for you."

Why would better be scary? Because change, in itself, is something my emotions are still learning how to process properly. My world has been shook up and turned upside down a time or two. I haven't known any sort of stability until these past few years, since

I was twelve. God is the only solid ground I have ever known. And it feels as if I have known Him forever and that we just met all at the same time.

HE HAS PATIENCE WITH ME

Every day I fear waking up one morning and Him just deciding to no longer communicate with me. I fear abandonment from my precious God. How will I ever not fear being abandoned from my future husband?

I naturally have these fears. I have learned through counseling not to act upon them. My fear isn't causing me to break down crying or believe the fears to be true. I have learned through professional counseling that my fears are not necessarily reality. They are triggers. They are reminders that life has not always been perfect.

God is not agitated with me that I have these fears. He knows the things I have been through, and He knows why they exist. He knows I have been trying so hard for so long. He knows my heart. He knows me. He is my example of what my future husband's love will be.

ONE WISH

If I knew I was going to die today and was granted one wish, I would wish for everyone to fall in love with Him. It took me writing a book to deeply connect with Him. Everyone's story is different. But, that's our love story.

MORE OF OUR LOVE

It's often just enough to be with someone. I don't need to touch them. Not even talk. A feeling passes between you both. You're not alone.

Marilyn Monroe

LETTER BETWEEN US

I should've been looking to You all this time to tell me what I'm worth. All the years I have lived with low self-esteem is unfortunate. I would've never felt or heard the words "slut" and "expendable" from You. I would've heard:

You are my cherished one. I've set you apart because I find you so special. You have always been mine, even when you ran away. Can't you see? I refused to let you go. You mean that much. You are that valuable.

And all those times you have been abused and mistreated, my heart was breaking just like the man I placed in your life to be your father, until you came home. You should've been taken care of. I'm sorry you suffered.

But you are making me proud for looking at the bright side. You get to help others by sharing your story and glorifying me in the process. And the gifts I have given you were given to you because I knew they would assist you in pursuing your calling once you were ready. Your story was predestined. Didn't you know?

Your calling, my dear, is to bless and touch other's hearts with your written words for the rest of your days. That is your purpose you have been searching for. Remember when I answered, "Wait" to your prayers last year? Yes, that was me.

You should get familiar with my voice because you will be hearing more from me now that all the noise in your life is gone. Let's keep it that way, please.

And so you know, I only waited until you were ready to reveal all of this to you. I did that because a father knows what's best. And guess what time it is?

The time is now. My beloved, you are ready for all that will be sent your way.

And don't worry, my Spirit will walk you through this. Every step of the way, I will be your guide. You and me until the end.

Love,
Your best friend

OUR FIRST STORY

One night over a year ago, I was reading in the book of Psalms. I felt led to underline parts that meant something to me. I would underline a phrase of a verse up to a whole verse. I did this for over twenty chapters. After I did that, I felt led to put them together in the exact order in which I had underlined them. When I had reviewed what I had written, it read a story. Here was my story at that time in my life:

> "He brought them out of darkness and the deepest gloom and broke away their chains. He stilled the storm to a whis-

per, the waves of the sea were hushed. Out of the goodness of your love, deliver me. I am poor and needy, and my heart is wounded within me. Let them know that it is your hand that you, O Lord, have done it. I love the Lord, for he heard my voice; he heard my cry for mercy, because he turned his ear to me, I will call on him as long as I live. The Lord protects the simplehearted; when I was in great need, he saved me. Be at rest once more, O my soul, for the Lord has been good to you. Save me, for I am yours. Therefore, I hate every wrong path. I wait for the Lord, my soul waits, and in his word I put my hope. But I have stilled and quieted my soul; like a weaned child with its mother, like a weaned child is my soul within me."

Psalm 107-131, NIV

After I read my "story," I decided to post it as a quote on my Facebook. I don't feel comfortable calling all my friends up witnessing to them about Jesus. But I thought if I put it out there, it would be a way of witnessing because people would view my page like my book. So I posted it that night.

The very next morning, one of my friends texted me to tell me how inspiring she felt it was and thanked me for posting it. That girl was one of the people who came to my rescue the night of the "door incident." She also sat with me in the emergency room for over four hours while I had X-rays and a CAT scan the following day.

OUR SECOND POEM

Shortly after I wrote my story from Psalms, I was led to write Him a poem. The first one I wrote when I was nine, and I wrote my second one when I was twenty-four years old.

The "Dear God" Poem (written 2/12/2010)

When I am alone,
The struggles within me arise.

I dream and awake,
As another day has gone by.

I'm still driven for perfection,
Something that plagues my soul.

If only I truly realized,
How God can make me whole.

He wants me pure,
He wants me to heal.

He wants me to realize,
That not one bit of it was His will. (looking back it was, but it wasn't)

To my Healer,
I cry out.

To my Redeemer,
I call.

To the Lover of my soul,
I worship.

To the only one who loves perfectly,
I give it all.

To the one I loved as a little girl,
To the one who favors me with His blessings.

To the one who keeps me safe,
To His presence who is no longer missing!

Lord, teach me to love myself like you do,
Let me see me through your eyes.

Keep my heart open as I give it back to you,
Please sever unwanted ties.

Your work in me is far from complete,
For this is only the start.

For you promised me a bright future,
And the desires of my heart!

I love you God,
I will never forget what you've done and will continue to do.

Please also bless my family and friends,
And keep my love for you brand new.

I don't want my passion to die,
For you are my deepest desire.

Teach me to love you how you see fit,
I promise I will never ever tire.

I could go on and on,
This you already know

And so you know God...I welcome the tears,
The cleansing that's making me whole.

I commit my life to you,
Let my love and mercy for others grow.

I'm not sure what's next,
But your Holy Spirit will show.

Goodnight my true Father,
Good-bye to my pride.

Goodnight to the one who gave it all back...

Love,
Your Bride.

NO MORE WEARY, TEARY EYES, JUST SUNNY SKIES

> *"Come to me, all who labor and are heavy laden, and I will give you rest. Take my yoke upon you, and learn from me, for I am gentle and lowly in heart, and you will find rest for your souls. For my yoke is easy, and my burden is light."*
>
> Matthew 11:28-30, ESV

I have heard it said that pain has no memory. I completely disagree. I can't recreate that sickening feeling in my stomach, but I remember what it made me want to do. It made me wish I were dead. How could I not remember that?

REMEMBERING HIM

Although nothing from my past deeply pains me now, how can you forget your former days? You will heal. And you will hopefully get to a point where you feel like none of it ever even happened, even though your mind knows differently. That's called a miracle, praise God! But you will never fully forget. But would you want to?

I hope I never forget all that God delivered me from. My tears of relief are my little treasures. No one will ever know what I have felt inside but me and my God. My treasures are my moments here and there where I shed a tear or two of gratitude, sometimes for just simply the good feelings I have inside about myself and my overall existence. They are my tears of utter relief.

They are my little reminders of my victory over death and destruction with God by my side. I hope those tears never cease because they are more than special; they are sacred to me. I hope I never forget what all He has done for me. It's such a big deal.

As a healed person, I fear the memory of how bad the bad days were will be drowned out by all the light and happy days to come. No more weary, teary eyes for this woman. I'm scared that because of that, I won't appreciate Him as much. Good thing we are guaranteed trials and times where we will need to depend on Him throughout our life. I will continually have reason to praise and seek Him. Without Him, my life doesn't measure up.

I don't want the passion I have for Him to die. I am in love, and I want it to last. I don't want my God to ever feel like I only used Him to get better. I don't want to forget any bit of how He saved me, over and over again. Just like I prayed for Him to give me the desire that He wanted me to have for Him, I have prayed that He doesn't ever let me forget—not even a little bit.

OTHER PURSUITS

During the time I didn't see my dad from ages fifteen to twenty-one, every time I would get coked up, I would think about him and dwell on the fact that he was being distant. Oftentimes, I would call him. "That night" I was finally finished with coke, I waited until it was time that I thought he would be up getting ready for work, around 6:00 or 7:00 a.m., to call. He answered and we spoke briefly, which was only a brief fix. Simply communicating with my dad was a fix. How sad.

I was always calling, always pursuing this dream that I would one day get my dad back. I went to a psychic once, and she told me it wasn't going to happen because the bridge had already been burned. I truly believed I would live the rest of my life without him. Just like I thought I was a lost cause, so was the dream of having a dad again.

Let's paint the picture clearly, I rejected him first. I was a horrible daughter, leaving him once just before Father's Day because a boyfriend wanted me to come back. I broke up with that boyfriend less than two weeks later because he was suffocating me.

Commitment is scary at twenty-five, let alone fifteen. It seems the more I pull away, the more the other person pursues. I have been on both ends of that. I was convinced I cared for the person because I was fighting to win them over. When the truth of the matter was, the rejection I felt from not being wanted only triggered my insecurities.

If I could just get him to like me back, I felt the problem would be solved. That nagging feeling would then disappear. But once I won him over, it was on to the next to say, "You are worthy."

Because that's what the guys wanting me said. When someone wants to be with you, doesn't that say "You mean something" and "You are someone to me, you are not nothing"? That is why relationships were one of my drugs when I was empty and felt like nothing. Relationships took the empty feelings away. That is why I put up with abuse at twenty-one from one guy and the other at seventeen.

HAPPY, HEALTHY, WHOLE

Being healthy is the goal. Healthy, happy, and wholeness go together. No whole person puts up with abuse.

It was a horrible position to be in when I felt like I couldn't live without a person or a drug. Thank God I am finally free!

HIS LOVE

His love is powerful. That is why there are so many love songs written to Him. I know what His love that He pours out all over me on a daily basis has done for me. He makes the hole go away. Mine was so big, He put me in a three-day trance to fill it once and for all. I have been in love ever since.

He filled me higher in my heart than acid, cocaine, and higher than any honeymoon phase of a relationship. I believe He did that to show me His power. He knew it would make me fall for Him. He knew that is what it would take to sweep me off my feet completely. It made me feel pursued and fought over.

He won this girl's heart back. It makes me feel like a treasure, regardless of my past, that our God of the universe loves me that much. He is giving me visions and books, and one day the man I want, as long as the desire stays in my heart. And I feel like I don't deserve any of it. But obviously I do, since He seems to think so.

Nowadays, I don't have to shed any more tears over boys and put up with being mistreated in order to feel like I am less alone in this world. I don't have to put up with feeling used emotionally, either. When you are always there for someone when they call, text, and/or send you e-mails, but you don't have the same access to them, you are allowing yourself to be used emotionally.

HIS PROMISE

He can't guarantee people won't ever hurt me again. He can't guarantee I will never feel pain and heartache again. But He promises to never leave me or forsake me. That is in several different books of the Bible, Old and New Testament.

I held in so much pain from my childhood it was keeping me from being a woman. My emotional maturity was that of the wounded little girl since I was still suppressing what she didn't know how to process when everything hurt her at once. The little girl I once was shut down on herself and all that mattered.

That is why I felt nothing for so long. I turned my back on God and then I shut down on myself and my emotions. My tears come from all ages. If I didn't grieve over what was I could never enter my future free of the burdens weighing me down. My Jesus is so good to me. And that is the same Jesus we all have access to, our Father's son who died so we can be directly linked to God and forgiven of our sins because He paid the price. No games or guessing, we are His and we have complete access to Him.

WANT HIM

Falling in love with God has been the most natural thing that has ever happened to me. He has always been there waiting, and we have had a couple of close calls, so it's not as if I fell in love with a stranger. He was my friend, first, for a long time. He did a lot of things for me, and He went to great lengths to pursue me.

I don't believe I was ever ready for His fullness until now. That is why He waited to truly show His power in my life. Because He knew when that happened, I would be sold-out to Him. And He knew that I needed to be healed before I could help other people.

Is a "God trip" an everyday or weekend thing for me? No, unfortunately not because He knows I would never leave my house if that were the case. He wants me to live my life on earth while I am here because I have the rest of eternity to spend with Him.

Webster defines want as: to feel a need or desire for; to wish for. True love cannot be found where it truly does not exist, and it cannot be hidden where it truly does. You can't deny a want for something more. Your want is not going to go away. A seed has just been planted in your heart if you haven't already given your life to Him. Rest assured, He is at work to pursue you right now.

And once He has won you over, you won't be able to hide or deny it. You will see why nothing else fit you in the past. You will then see, as I saw, why no other attempt at your search was ever fulfilled. And that is when you'll know what I know. Then you will share what you've went through for the sake of others without hesitation.

When you realize that He had everything to do with you getting out of your pit and getting fully recovered (if that is where you find yourself), you will see. You will not be victorious without Him—not in the way that I have been. Victory is your soul being free.

I desired complete freedom.

It all came together for me very recently. I have finally arrived to a place where there is no more straddling the fence being who you want me to be, whoever you are. I am called to be who He wants me to be. And that is better than any version of myself I could ever be on my own. Who my Creator and Finisher has called me to be is also superior to any me I have ever made myself into, only to accommodate what you wanted from me, whoever you were at the time. I finally get that my worth and validation does not come from anyone but my Savior.

Satan wanted to keep my dark parts hidden; he didn't want me to get real with myself. He wanted to keep me in bondage, and he knew what would happen once light was exposed on the broken parts. For when the light hit them, I saw my mistakes for what they were in God's eyes, and I finally found my freedom within that truth.

"Then you will know the truth, and the truth will set you free" (John 8:32, NIV).

Dying to self and getting real is not easy. It may be unattractive. There are moments where some people say, unless they understand like I and many others out there do, that parts of recovery appear unusual.

Lots of tears were shed during my process. I screamed my heart out. While lying on the floor crying out to God, I kicked my feet like a child throwing a fit. If only someone had a video camera during all of this, they could be making some money. But guess what? At the end of all of that, I found my freedom I had been searching for. Let me be your living proof that freedom is possible if you can't be your own just yet. God loves you. And God loves you through me, too.

NOTE FROM THE AUTHOR

The first time I actually said, "Lord, draw near to me," was the previous Sunday before I began writing you. It was surreal, but nothing compared to our "weekend getaway" that was to come. I had my head down and eyes closed when I saw a brief image of a scroll. I also saw the guy I have had a little girl crush on for over a year with a gold wedding band on. That will be left open to interpretation for the time being.

When I started crying at work that Friday, it wasn't out of the norm for me just yet. Then I decided to start writing while crying, which was a first. And other than meeting one of my girlfriends for coffee after work, I didn't stop writing that weekend.

I came home and wrote. I woke up at 7:00 a.m. on a Saturday morning and wrote some more, went to work for a few voluntary overtime hours, and came home and wrote until I went to bed, totaling ten hours. That Sunday, I wrote from 7:00 a.m. until 2:00 a.m., which was a total of seventeen hours. I was clearly on a mission.

Remember my "vision" or "dream" of the scroll? It was in dream colors and format. I am new to His spiritual "presents," so I don't know which name is more appropriate at this time. I do know I thought nothing more of the "scroll" until Sunday night. I took a break to pray and seek God, and it hit me. Books used to be written on scrolls.

I thought it was going to be my first published book even before I recalled the scroll. I never heard God speak to me in the way He was doing that weekend. God told me my story was a part of His plan, and it was going to help others. He also told me that He would put together the broken pieces. He told me that my past would serve a purpose. These are thoughts my mind could have never conjured up. And if I was going to subconsciously create my own vision of a book, I would have dreamed up a book—not a scroll. Trust me, I have analyzed all the possibilities.

I won't ever feel as if I deserve credit for this book or any of my books to come. God placed them in my heart. That initial message that was spread out from the beginning of this book until the end was for the books I will write to the hurting, the ones whom I have felt their pain. And the truth is we have all hurt in some way. So my books are to all of us, you and me.

I felt led to elaborate on the message by going into some great detail about my past. I felt like God was telling me to open my heart to everyone and be real. I wrote, thinking God was going to have the whole world read it as soon as it was finished. I cried my heart out that whole weekend for two reasons: I was not only real with the reader, which was terrifying in itself, I was real with myself for the first time since things started going wrong for me at twelve years old.

People needed to know what happened in my life that led me to where I found myself. I knew there were many out there who could relate. This was my story through my eyes. The story will never change. What happened, who I hurt, who hurt me, what I did wrong, who wronged me—none of that can be erased.

Even though the whole world has not read my book, it doesn't matter because I have already gone through the motions as if they have. The scariest part is over. Now my thoughts are, *Why did God wait so long to prompt me to do this?* And I already know the answer. It is always about timing. And our loving God always knows best.

Friend,

If you've read this book, here is the thing. When judgment day comes, you won't have an excuse. You won't be able to say you were never told. Did you know that Charles Darwin, the one who created the idea of evolution, died a professed Christian? Don't waste your years and wait until you realize your life is ending to seek Him.

Your potential salvation is the reason why I have done what many people may not understand by giving the contents of my heart away to strangers. I recently discovered how real He is and also how big of a deal salvation is. And if I know there is something I can do to help you and I don't, I know I will be judged for that. My conscience is clear, the chains are broken, and I'm finally free—all with one stone. This book turned me into a woman at the age of twenty-five. I sure hope it did something for you too. If it only helped or inspired one person, it has been worth my while.

I know the value of being real. I know what genuine has always meant to me. God is calling me to write for the rest of my life. Writing will be my career, and writing is my passion.

Although my voice is going to change throughout the years as I mature and I go from single to married to Mom, I will always be here for you in this way as long as I am alive. We can all grow together, and you will make it through whatever you are going through with Him by your side. And I hope me reaching out is an added bonus.

Since I am not a licensed counselor, I won't feel comfortable dialoguing with you one-on-one. However, I will read, pray for you, and answer all of your questions in book form. Send your e-mails to FreeToBeMinistries@gmail.com, and I will add you to my list that I will write to everyday in order to help edify and lift your spirits.

He is expanding my vision for my future ministry on a daily basis. My next step is to attend a Bible college to learn more about the things I do not know in His living and breathing Word. Since that would require me to quit my full-time job with benefits to attend, I believe this book was written to provide me with a source of income while I gain a degree in Christian ministries and also to touch hearts with you. How could I hate my past now? My past is what has brought us together. Thank you for reading.

Until next time,
Celia

"CELIA'S EYES"

BY AMY DOCKERY

It depends on what she wears
Sometimes her eyes are sapphires
Then other times they're more like emerald green
God I hate to stare
But there's something so much deeper
There's inner beauty like I've never seen

Cause Celia's eyes are windows to her soul
Where a little girl with broken dreams has found a hand to hold
Like a loving daddy You'll make everything alright
And God there's so much beauty
That lies beyond the beauty
God I can see what You see in Celia's eyes

She's wise beyond her years
From a life of rejection
But it's amazing how the trials have made her strong
Sometimes she fights back tears
From all the pain she's been through
But she knows You can make right from wrong

And her eyes are stained glass windows to her soul
A heart of an angel—heaven only knows
All the hurt and sorrow
Your touch is making right
God I can see the beauty
That lies beyond the beauty
God I can see what You see in Celia's eyes

Now Celia's eyes reflect tender love
Healing, grace and mercy from above....
And all the hurt and sorrow
Your touch is making right
Oh I can see the beauty
That lies beyond the beauty
God I can see what You see in Celia's eyes
Yes I can see what You see in Celia's eyes